Cambridge Elements

Elements in the Psychology of Religion
edited by
Jonathan Lewis-Jong
St Mary's University Twickenham and University of Oxford

MORALITY AND THE GODS

Benjamin Grant Purzycki
Aarhus University

Shaftesbury Road, Cambridge CB2 8EA, United Kingdom

One Liberty Plaza, 20th Floor, New York, NY 10006, USA

477 Williamstown Road, Port Melbourne, VIC 3207, Australia

314–321, 3rd Floor, Plot 3, Splendor Forum, Jasola District Centre, New Delhi – 110025, India

103 Penang Road, #05–06/07, Visioncrest Commercial, Singapore 238467

Cambridge University Press is part of Cambridge University Press & Assessment, a department of the University of Cambridge.

We share the University's mission to contribute to society through the pursuit of education, learning and research at the highest international levels of excellence.

www.cambridge.org
Information on this title: www.cambridge.org/9781009598729

DOI: 10.1017/9781009414036

© Benjamin Grant Purzycki 2025

This publication is in copyright. Subject to statutory exception and to the provisions of relevant collective licensing agreements, no reproduction of any part may take place without the written permission of Cambridge University Press & Assessment.

When citing this work, please include a reference to the DOI 10.1017/9781009414036

First published 2025

A catalogue record for this publication is available from the British Library

ISBN 978-1-009-59872-9 Hardback
ISBN 978-1-009-41402-9 Paperback
ISSN 2753-6866 (online)
ISSN 2753-6858 (print)

Cambridge University Press & Assessment has no responsibility for the persistence or accuracy of URLs for external or third-party internet websites referred to in this publication and does not guarantee that any content on such websites is, or will remain, accurate or appropriate.

For EU product safety concerns, contact us at Calle de José Abascal, 56, 1°, 28003 Madrid, Spain, or email eugpsr@cambridge.org

Morality and the Gods

Elements in the Psychology of Religion

DOI: 10.1017/9781009414036
First published online: June 2025

Benjamin Grant Purzycki
Aarhus University

Author for correspondence: Benjamin Grant Purzycki, bgpurzycki@cas.au.dk

Abstract: The relationship between religion and morality has been a steadfast topic of inquiry for centuries. This Element probes how the social sciences have addressed this relationship by detailing how theory and method have evolved over the past few generations. Sections 1 and 2 examine the historical roots of cross-cultural inquiry, and Section 3 introduces the empirical tools developed to address cross-cultural patterns statistically. Sections 4–6 probe how the contemporary evolutionary social sciences have been addressing the role religious cognition, behavior, and beliefs play on moral conduct. By critically examining the tools and theories specifically developed to answer questions about the evolution of morality, society, and the gods, this Element shows that much of our current knowledge about this relationship has been significantly shaped by our cultural history as a field. It argues that the relationship between religion and morality is, despite considerable diversity in form, quite common around the world.

Keywords: morality, religion, evolution of religion, evolution of cooperation, cross-cultural research

© Benjamin Grant Purzycki 2025

ISBNs: 9781009598729 (HB), 9781009414029 (PB), 9781009414036 (OC)
ISSNs: 2753-6866 (online), 2753-6858 (print)

Contents

1	Introduction	1
2	History and Ethnography	2
3	Societal Typologies and the Quantification of Culture	12
4	Cognition and Religion	25
5	The Evolution of Religious Behavior	38
6	The Evolution of Religious Beliefs	49
7	Conclusion	62
	References	64

1 Introduction

The relationship between morality[1] and the gods[2] has been a steadfast topic of discussion for at least as long as the written word. In fact, the earliest of preserved written records explicitly mention a relationship between prescribed moral rules and what the gods want. Written around the twenty-first century BCE, the oldest known legal code – the Sumerian Ur-Nammu code – claims inspiration from the gods. Inscribed 400 years later, the Code of Hammurabi begins with references to the gods Anu and Bel. In addition to reporting that Anu and Bel assigned the task of overseeing humanity to another god, Marduk, Hammurabi suggests that they also commanded him to promote his laws and to "destroy the wicked and the evil." In claiming these gods encouraged him to "prevent the strong from oppressing the weak" (Harper, 1904, 3), Hammurabi links gods, the moral order, and equality together in ways researchers have theorized since the dawn of the social sciences.

These documents explicitly connect the gods to moral codes, but many questions arise when we treat the nature of this relationship as a social scientific question. For instance, how common is the connection between the gods and morality? Is it present across the world's religions or is it particular to a narrow subset of religious traditions? How is the connection expressed? Is it found in both beliefs and behavior? Does religion actually contribute to moral behavior or is it just a matter of how people talk? How should we even conceive religion and morality? Why associate gods with how we treat each other? This Element addresses these questions and how the social sciences and other fields have gone about addressing them.[3]

This Element is outlined as follows. Section 2 details the deeper history of thought regarding the relationship between religion and morality. In doing so, it highlights important representative shifts in thinking and method and examines some of the forces that propelled the emergence of anthropological and sociological inquiry. These fields increased our knowledge of the kinds of cultural diversity exhibited by people around the world and created the demand

---

[1] This Element does not defend a particular definition of "morality." For the sake of exposition and further comparison, it instead compares authors' uses on their own terms. Throughout the text, I'll include explicit definitions and examples when they are available. See Section 4.2.1 for a concise survey of some important views.

[2] This text treats "gods" and "spirits" synonymously as concepts of anthropomorphic, superempirical spiritual entities. While spiritual forces like *karma*, *mana*, and *luck* might also play an important role on morality, it remains unclear if such forces affect human relationships any differently than gods (see Sørensen & Purzycki, 2023; C. J. White et al., 2019).

[3] All data and code used herein can be accessed here: https://github.com/bgpurzycki/Morality andtheGods.

for global, cross-cultural models and methods. Section 3 critically assesses the development of cross-cultural typologies and datasets, two pivotal resources that have had a lasting impact on how we see the relationship between morality, society, and the gods. In Section 4, we'll then examine the contemporary cognitive and psychological sciences, fields of which have emphasized the importance of the biological foundations of morality and religious beliefs. Drawing from this, we'll see how the scientific study of religious behaviors (Section 5) and beliefs (Section 6) embraced contemporary evolutionary theory. The concluding section offers some summary points and a survey of the horizon ahead.

2 History and Ethnography

We might never know just how long human beings have contemplated how the divine relates to how they should interact with each other (see Rossano, 2010).[4] As we saw, the oldest known writing clearly notes this relationship, but it most likely long predates writing. Interestingly, the earliest accounts of the New World's indigenous populations include details of their religious traditions and moral sensibilities. These observations provide us with a glimpse of how the West's ongoing fascination with morality and the gods evolved. As we'll see, the more European observers interacted with non-Western populations, the greater the demand to account for human variation became. Central to this increased demand was the topic of morality and the gods.

2.1 Contact

The earliest written European observations of indigenous, "traditional," or "non-state" populations[5] include some striking claims about religion. For example, in his diary, Christopher Columbus suggested that the native Taíno (Arawak) "would become Christians very easily, for it seemed to [him] that they had no religion" (Dunn & Kelley Jr., 1989, 69). A more nuanced view comes from Dominican friar Bartolomé de las Casas (1484–1566). Working in the New World throughout the 1500s, de las Casas agreed that American Indians lacked the "true faith" of Christianity, but argued that they would have no trouble learning it because they were so reasonable. In fact, de las Casas devoted much of his life to demonstrating that American natives were

---

[4] This section draws from Purzycki and McKay (2023) and Lightner, Bendixen, and Purzycki (2023).
[5] Outside of direct quotation, I'll use "indigenous," "traditional," or "non-state" henceforth to refer to the religious systems found in relatively smaller-scale societies of non-European descent.

remarkably virtuous and their societies were diverse and socially complex in ways that matched or even surpassed the ancient civilizations so often adored by the West:

> Did Plato, Socrates, Pythagoras, or even Aristotle leave us better or more natural or more necessary exhortations to the virtuous life than these barbarians delivered to their children? Does the Christian religion teach us more, save the faith and what it teaches us of invisible and supernatural matters? Therefore, no one may deny that these people are fully capable of governing themselves and of living like men of good intelligence and more than others well ordered, sensible, prudent, and rational. (cited in Hanke, 1951, 80)

Here, de las Casas rhetorically asks whether Christianity really does contain much of anything in the way of being a good person beyond what American Indians already taught their children. He also notes that the virtues to which he refers are those necessary for self-governance; American Indians already know all that is required to have self-sustaining societies. Alas, not all missionaries agreed and de las Casas remains a notable exception.

Nearly a century and a half later, two missionaries working among the native Martiniquez islanders left some curious insights into their method. One missionary suggested that "having lived without any knowledge of God, [the native Caribbeans] die without hope of salvation. *It would be better for us to say that they have no religion at all*, instead of describing as a cult of divinity all their trifling nonsense, superstitions, or more exactly sacrileges with which they honor all of the demons who seduce them" (Breton, 1929 [1635–1647], 5, emphasis added). Another (Bouton, 1635) concurs, noting that the indigenous "do not trouble themselves with knowing what becomes of [the souls of the dead]; at least we have never been able to draw this information out of them" (1). Conveying the level of methodological sophistication of the time, Bouton notes that he and his fellow missionaries have had very little experience with the people, suggesting that they could perhaps "learn more if we were to live among them or they among us. At the present time they are greatly separated from us by inaccessible hills, so that we see them rarely and only when they come by sea to trade with the French" (Bouton, 1635).

Two hundred years later, one missionary who worked among the Abipón Indians of Paraguay held that "the American savages are slow, dull, and stupid in the apprehension of things not present to their outward senses. Reasoning is a process troublesome and almost unknown to them. It is, therefore, no wonder that the contemplation of terrestrial or celestial objects should inspire them with no idea of the creative Deity, nor indeed of any thing heavenly" (Dobrizhoffer, 1822, 58). Even after spending eighteen years (1749–1767) among the Abipón, he maintained that they are "accustomed from their earliest age to superstition, slaughter, and rapine, and naturally dull and stupid as brutes." Yet, in striking contrast to de las Casas' sentiments, he notes that these "fools, idiots, and madmen" (64) are nevertheless capable of conversion "when the good sense of the teacher compensates for the stupidity of his pupils" (62).

These days, we might be considerably less credulous about past generations' unsavory conclusions about indigenous peoples and their religions. If we are genuinely interested in what the religions of traditional societies are/were like and whether they were associated with morality, these authors' motivations and worrisome methods (or lack thereof) should give us pause. Things have changed. The more the West interacted with the rest of the world, the more it had to come to terms with the dazzling variation that people exhibited. Eventually, the field of anthropology offered an antidote to the bigotry of generations past, thus paving the way for a more enlightened view and approach to understanding cultural variation. As we'll see, however, these contributions did not come overnight. In fact, we're still in the midst of the transition.

2.2 The Dawn of Professional Cross-Cultural Comparison

Professional anthropology developed as a means to come to grips with the West's increasing awareness of humans' remarkable diversity (Harris, 1968). While fieldwork and direct inquiry took some time to become standard, the quest to understand the underlying commonalities of humanity amid our overwhelming variation was central to the field's origins. In fact, anthropology's genesis was specifically devoted to coming to terms with religious diversity.

In the earliest days of the discipline, researchers were motivated by a few competing cultural evolutionary theories. One was progressivism. A prototypical model of progressivism comes from early anthropologist Lewis Henry Morgan (1877), who argued that "mankind commenced their career at the bottom of the scale and worked their way up...through the slow accumulations of experimental knowledge" (3). The stages of this scale were threefold, including savagery, barbarism, and civilization, each of which have "lower," "middle," and "upper" designations.[6] Across these progressive stages, subsistence – or the way people procure food – "has been increased and perfected," languages were increasingly articulate, and there was an increased cultural emphasis on private

---

[6] Morgan was not the first to deploy such terms. In fact, in his defense of American Indians, Bartolomé de las Casas creates a fourfold typology of barbarism. American Indians, he writes, are merely the kinds of barbarians who are non-numerate, non-literate, and lack Christianity rather than those who are irrational or ferocious and violent (cited in Sanderlin, 1992, 123–127).

property (5–6).[7] In this view, cultural evolution was progressive; civilization was obviously inherently better than savagery. But this model of evolution was also unilinear; to become civilized, a society must have passed through a state of barbarism. Morgan's view also offered a mechanism of change; humanity's constant tinkering and drive for improvement contributed to a society's passage from one state to another. Indigenous peoples in relatively smaller societies evidently hadn't tinkered enough.

It was in this progressivist milieu that came what is often hailed as the founding document of anthropology, namely, E. B. Tylor's two-volume *Primitive Culture* (1871a, 1871b). Drawing from a wide range of cross-cultural observations – albeit of the time's quality – Tylor's work disputed the then-held conviction that indigenous societies lack religion. This bears repeating: Tylor spent two volumes arguing, among other things, against the centuries-old idea that "primitive peoples" had no religion.

Like Morgan, Tylor viewed the development of societies as progressive, considering that "the savage state in some measure represents an early condition of mankind, out of which the higher culture has gradually been developed or evolved, by processes still in regular operation as of old, the result showing that, on the whole, progress has far prevailed over relapse" (32). Despite this tendency toward progression, so-called "higher culture" nevertheless contains what Tylor called "survivals," that is, "processes, customs, opinions, and so forth, which have been carried on by force of habit into a new state of society different from that in which they had their original home, and they thus remain as proofs and examples of an older condition of culture out of which a newer has been evolved" (16). So, while societies might progressively evolve from "lower" to "higher," there remain vestiges of "lower" traditions in the "higher" populations. One such survival is animism, "the doctrine of souls and other spiritual beings in general" (23). In Tylor's view, animism is the essence of religion and he spent hundreds of pages addressing the prospect that belief in spiritual beings might be found in all "stages" of cultural evolution.

Despite all of this attention and effort, in a matter of a few short passages, Tylor simply dismisses the possibility that the animism of the "lower" traditions includes a moral component, maintaining that "lower animism is not immoral,

---

[7] Incidentally, Morgan does not discuss religion that much, but does characterize "all primitive religions [as] grotesque and to some extent unintelligible" (5). Given the context, we might generously take "grotesque" to mean strange and/or haphazard. He also notes that some American Indian traditions were "more or less vague and indefinite, and loaded with crude superstitions. Element worship can be traced among the principal tribes, with a tendency to polytheism in the advanced tribes" (115). This is one early take on the relationship between a society's structure and its religious worldview.

it is unmoral" and is "almost devoid of that ethical element which to the educated modern mind is the very mainspring of practical religion" (Tylor, 1871b, 360). Further:

> One great element of religion, that moral element which among the higher nations forms its most vital part, is indeed little represented in the religion of the lower races. It is not that these races have no moral sense or no moral standard, for both are strongly marked among them, if not in formal precept, at least in that traditional consensus of society which we call public opinion, according to which certain actions are held to be good or bad, right or wrong. It is that the conjunction of ethics and Animistic philosophy, so intimate and powerful in the higher culture, seems scarcely yet to have begun in the lower. (Tylor, 1871a, 427)

After appealing to a simple lack of evidence, Tylor reminds us of the virtues of the synthesis of ethics – "actions held to be good or bad, right or wrong" – and animism found in "higher culture." Models of the good and bad are separate from the religions of the "lower" cultures.

Tylor suggests that this separation accounts for another primary contrast between "savage" and modern religions, namely, their views of death. Here, the adherents of modern religions believe that where one goes after death is contingent on what one does in this life (the "retribution-doctrine") whereas traditional religions simply go to another place (the "continuance-doctrine"):

> Looking at religion from a political point of view, as a practical influence on human society, it is clear that among its greatest powers has been its divine sanction of ethical laws, its theological enforcement of morality, its teaching of moral government of the universe, its supplanting the 'continuance-doctrine' of a future life by the 'retribution-doctrine' supplying moral motive in the present. But such alliance belongs almost wholly to religions above the savage level, not to the earlier and lower creeds. (Tylor, 1871b, 361)

Here, Tylor notes that religion can have "a practical influence on human society," the "greatest" of which is bolstering the moral order. Believing in an afterlife that is based on what you do in this life was one such mechanism bolstering the social order, a mechanism that exists "almost wholly" in societies that have risen above states of savagery.

Again, it is not the case that Tylor denied that indigenous peoples lacked a moral sense. He emphatically holds that both religion *and* morality are human universals. Furthermore, it was not the case that Tylor saw no relationship between religion and society at all. In fact, he suggests that "Among nation after nation it is still clear how…human society and government became the model on which divine society and government were shaped" (Tylor, 1871b, 248). Presaging later views (see Section 3), Tylor suggests that the structure of a society's religious worldview is a reflection of their actual social world.

This betrays Tylor's intellectualism, the view that religion functions to help explain the world. In particular, religion's role was to help people account for themselves.

So over the two volumes that gave birth to a new academic field, Tylor managed to dismantle the then-prevalent idea that traditional populations lack religion. He maintains the view that native religions do not "supply moral motives" that guide constituents' interactions with appeals to repercussions. This had to evolve independently or, as he argues elsewhere, learned from other "higher cultures" (Tylor, 1892). To the extent that progressivist theory influenced his views of religion, we can surmise that Tylor viewed the supplying of "moral motives" among the religions of those "above the savage level" as an improvement over those of the "earlier and lower creeds."

There was, however, some explicit resistance to Tylor's claims about "savage" or "primitive" religions and their connection to morality. For example, Andrew Lang – one of Tylor's students – was skeptical of his mentor's "high a priori line that savage minds are incapable of originating the notion of a moral Maker" (A. Lang, 1909, xiv). He did not argue against Tylor on the grounds that we should not consider entire cultural groups as having intrinsically better qualities than others. Rather, Lang endorsed a competing view, namely, the "degenerationist" or "devolutionary" theory. This theory posited that all humans were originally united in one common culture and all contemporary cultural diversity represents deviations from that common source (a religiously couched corollary of this view held that all of humanity were once united in Babylon and have since strayed). The goal of anthropology, then, was to search for the original cultural complex and examine how various traits had either maintained or dispensed with the original society's ways. Of course, this view has long since been discarded, as there is no evidence of such a culture and we know that modern humanity's common ancestors were foragers who lived in southern Africa some 300,000 years ago (Schlebusch et al., 2017).

In this devolutionary spirit, Lang pondered the possibility that beliefs in spiritual beings with "high moral attributes" might be one of Tylor's "survivals" of our original state and thus could have predated spirits and gods who play "silly or obscene tricks [or are] lustful and false" (xv). In other words, Lang saw beliefs in moralistic gods as not only common, but also indicative of humanity's once-united cultural state. Drawing upon his review of information about Australian Aboriginal traditions, he points to the "high moral attributes" of their deities, including one deity's moral precepts. Among them include prescriptions "To share everything they have with their friends" and "To live peaceably with their friends" (181).

Lang also argued against Tylor's view that "savage high gods" necessarily have their origins in cultural borrowings from "higher" cultures. To do this, he reviewed the then-extant cross-cultural evidence of traditions with gods thought to be models of morality and those believed to directly punish people for engaging in immoral behavior (193–210). Summarizing the state of the field at the time, Lang goes on the offensive: "Anthropology holds the certainly erroneous idea that the religion of the most backward races is always non-moral" (256). In notably stark terms, Lang indicts the then-prevailing view of the nascent field of anthropology. For different theoretical and methodological reasons, the social sciences grew to concur with Lang's conclusions.

For instance, one of the founders of modern sociology, Émile Durkheim (2001 [1912]) saw morality as a central component to both conceptions of the soul (194) and religion more generally. He even treated religion as a mechanism *for* society:

> No society can exist that does not feel the need at regular intervals to sustain and reaffirm the collective feelings and ideas that constitute its unity and its personality. Now, this moral remaking can be achieved only by means of meetings, assemblies, or congregations in which individuals, brought into close contact, reaffirm in common their common feelings: hence those ceremonies whose goals, results, and methods do not differ in kind from properly religious ceremonies. (322)

Here, Durkheim equates "morality" with a society's sense of "unity" and identity; morality is what holds societies together, makes them what and who they are. As complexes of regulatory practices and beliefs, Durkheim sees religion as a means by which societies maintain this sense of unity. As it includes mechanisms found in the secular world and organizes people into "meetings, assemblies, and congregations," religion forges moral bonds between people and can thus contribute to the sustainability of a society.

In summary, then, while Tylor saw no relationship between morality and "savage" religions, Lang saw this relationship manifest in beliefs about the gods and their espoused principles, and Durkheim saw it in the way religious institutions contribute to social solidarity. Over the next half century, anthropological consensus grew to side with the facts stressed by Lang and Durkheim, though having long-abandoned the theoretical commitments of Lang and Tylor. A confluence of new developments shaped the social scientific view of religion and morality, namely, ethnographic fieldwork, increased appreciation of the relationship between society and subsistence, and the commitment to understanding societies' traditions on their own terms.

2.3 Society, Function, and Fieldwork

In the 1930s, fueled by what a generation of ethnographic field researchers had learned directly from traditional people, celebrated anthropologist Bronislaw Malinowski witnessed and theorized the close association between religious beliefs, practice, and morality: "Every religion, primitive or developed, presents the three main aspects, dogmatic, ritual, and ethical…It is equally important to grasp the essential interrelation of these three aspects, to recognize that they are only really three facets of the same essential fact" (Malinowski, 2014, 134–135). Even commenting on how long it had taken scientists of humanity to come to terms with this, he expounds on this interrelation:

> That every organized belief implies a congregation, must have been felt by many thinkers instructed by scholarship and common sense. Yet…science was slow to incorporate the dictates of simple and sound reason…[that find] that worship always happens in common because it touches common concerns of the community. *And here…enters the ethical element intrinsically inherent in all religious activities. They always require efforts, discipline, and submission on the part of the individual for the good of the community.*
> (Malinowski, 2014, 137, emphasis added)

In this passage, Malinowski sees the relationship between morality and the gods as encoded in religious behavior. Here, he explicitly associates "worship" with exerting individual "effort, discipline, and submission" to benefit one's community; the "ethical element…inherent in all religious activities" contributes to the "good of the community." These contributions come at a cost to individuals – they take "efforts, discipline, and submission" and are therefore neither obviously nor immediately in individuals' immediate self-interest. As we'll see in Section 5, this economic emphasis of religion's costs and benefits has since become standard in some contemporary evolutionary views of religion. For now, let's attend to the theory underlying Malinowski's observations.

Generally, Malinowski sought to account for the rise and persistence of certain cultural traits. In his view, such traditions fulfill different needs. Defining function as the process of satisfying those needs (Malinowski, 1944, 159), he spells out an early functionalist theory of culture:

- "Culture is essentially an instrumental apparatus by which man is put in a position to better cope with the concrete specific problems that face him in his environment in the course of the satisfaction of his needs.
- "It is a system of objects, activities, and attitudes in which every part exists as a means to an end.

- "Such activities, attitudes and objects are organized around important and vital tasks into institutions such as family, the clan, the local community, the tribe, and the organized teams of economic coöperation, political, legal, and educational activity" (150)

Here, Malinowski asserts that culture is a tool with which people fix problems. Some of those challenges stem from social organization and domains such as economy, law, and education. Much like Durkheim's (2001 [1912]) view of religion as fulfilling the "need...[for society] to sustain and reaffirm the collective feelings and ideas that constitute its unity and its personality" (322), Malinowski saw religion as addressing "common concerns of the community" (Malinowski, 2014, 137). This conviction – and the theory underlying it – became standard for anthropology. The recognition of this inextricable link between morality and religion became so standard, in fact, that major voices in the field eventually treated it as self-evident.

Consider the sentiments of E. E. Evans-Pritchard (1965), the leading anthropologist of religion of his time. In a poignant critique of previous generations' efforts, he notes that:

> it was [once] held that primitive people must have the crudest religious conceptions...This may further be illustrated in the condescending argument, once it was ascertained beyond doubt that primitive peoples, even the hunters and collectors, have gods with high moral attributes, that they must have borrowed the idea, or just the word without comprehension of its meaning, from a higher culture, from missionaries, traders, and others...Modern research has shown that little value can be attributed to statements of this sort. (Evans-Pritchard, 1965, 107)

Here, Evans-Pritchard identifies the relationship between morality and the gods by their utility as models of morality and virtue. Not only does Evans-Pritchard acknowledge that small-scale foragers "have gods with high moral attributes," but he characterizes the view that they must have borrowed such a belief from outsiders as "condescending" (see Schebesta & Schütze, 1957, 1–10, for a detailed treatment of this issue).

Indeed, it is not difficult to find links of various kinds between religion and morality in the ethnographies of various societies around the world. A casual scan of ethnographic records suggests many hints and explicit accounts of gods having some association with behaviors that might be construed as "moral":

- the Inuit (global Arctic) Sedna myth is about the supernatural consequences of selfishness where white bears punish people for ancestral Inuits' moral transgressions (Turner, 1894, 261–262)
- the Siouan (American Great Plains) notion of *wakan tanka* (lit. sacred vastness) is recorded in 1896 as an omnipresent and omniscient entity interested in human behavior (Walker, 1980, 75) and Siouan religion is indigenously

characterized as forbidding "the [avaricious] accumulation of wealth and the enjoyment of luxury" (Eastman, 1911, 9)
- in Nuer society (East Africa), "such moral faults as meanness, disloyalty, dishonesty, slander, lack of deference to seniors, and so forth, cannot be entirely dissociated from sin, for God may punish them even if those who have suffered from them take no action of their own account" (Evans-Pritchard, 1956, 193)
- Paliyan (South India) gods are believed to "punish incest, theft, or murder with an accident or illness" (Gardner, 1972, 434)
- a G/wi (Southern Africa) god's "anger is expected if some taboos are broken and as a result of certain acts...in order to show man's lack of arrogance and thereby to avoid [N!adima's] displeasure...Death and other misfortunes are sometimes attributed to his anger" (Silberbauer, 1972, 319)
- some members of the related Dobe Ju/'hoansi report that spirits "expect certain behavior of us. We must eat so, and act so. When you are quarrelsome and unpleasant to other people, and people are angry with you, the *//gangwasi* see this and come to kill you. The *//gangwasi* can judge who is right and who is wrong" (Lee, 2003, 129–130)
- among the Dogrib (Canadian Northwest), "Wrongdoing [e.g., 'slacker[s], womanizer[s], and other transgressors of...norms'] might incur the visitation of supernatural illness" (Helm, 1972, 79)
- elements of moralistic punishment are in Matsigenkan (northwestern South America) folktales (Izquierdo, Johnson, and Shepard Jr, 2008; A. Johnson, 2003).

For at least two reasons, none of them would surprise the likes of Malinowski and Evans-Pritchard. First, they witnessed theorized the moral content and/or function of traditional religions first-hand and theorized about it. Second, they would appreciate that these observations come from ethnographic fieldwork, synthetic anthropological works, and directly from indigenous people themselves rather than explorers, missionaries, and armchair anthropologists. Even if these were exceptional views, the content of these observations nevertheless run counter to the strong sentiments of early missionaries and social theorists like Tylor.

So, the first century of anthropology included a debate about how central and universal morality was in the religious sphere. Even contemporaneous researchers with access to the same ethnographic record achieved remarkably divergent views, often even drawing from the same theoretical orientation. How then would we go about reasonably reconciling these views?

From a methodological perspective, we could be skeptical about any position; both generalize about a wide range of traditional societies and it is easy to make sweeping generalizations or cherry-pick examples to substantiate one's views. The essential question here, then, is how safe such conclusions are. Framed probabilistically, the question becomes: *what is the likelihood that a small-scale society links morality to their religious tradition?* To address this question, the subsequent generation of social scientists developed cross-cultural datasets. As we'll see, these resources allowed researchers to assess global patterns of culture, thus bringing a more systematic empirical approach to bear on such debates. However, they also carried considerable baggage that subsequent generations unfortunately inherited.

3 Societal Typologies and the Quantification of Culture

In their quest to understand human variation, previous generations developed standards for documenting and theorizing about the world's cultural traditions.[8] As this documentation increased in detail and sophistication, researchers increasingly abandoned the erroneous conceits of progressive models of cultural evolution. The more cross-cultural data anthropologists accumulated, the less satisfying casual observation and hasty generalizations became. Newer, more nuanced models linked cultural traits together. Furthermore, theory steadily became more inclined to examine traditions in light of the functions they served and the processes that contributed to their development.

Are there common cultural traditions found around the world? What explains them? Are some kinds of societies more likely to have some specific cultural traits than others? Why? With the expectations of rigorously collected ethnographic data and a global perspective afforded by the belvedere of academia, researchers began to categorize societies and cultural traits in discrete and formally comparable ways. This facilitated the quantitative study of sociocultural evolution. As we'll see, the link between religion and morality played a major role in the development of these tools.

3.1 Societal Typologies

Societal typologies subsequent to those of Morgan and Tylor grounded human organization in a society's economy. Rather than the gradual trial-and-error improvement of making a living as suggested in previous models, newer approaches explained many cultural traits by virtue of the way societies made a living. One influential model came from Elman Service (1962), who discussed four society types – bands, tribes, chiefdoms, and states (Table 1). These society types were linked to subsistence; bands are foragers, tribes engage in horticulture or herding (pastoralism), agriculturalists tend toward chiefdoms, and industrialized states typically have market economies. In this model,

---

[8] This section draws from Lightner et al. (2023), Purzycki and McKay (2023), and Purzycki and Watts (2018).

Table 1 Service's model of societal variation with Wallace's corresponding religious types. Economic specialization increases from bands to states. Note that population sizes are inferred based on Service's discussion throughout the text (see pp. 58–59).

type	economy	pop. size	decisions	religion
band	foraging	25–100	egalitarian	shamanic
tribe	hort./herding	≈ 500	collective	communal
chiefdom	agriculture	> 500	representative	Olympian
state	industrial	lots	top-down	monotheistic

the domestication of food represents a primary mechanism for increasing population size. The intensification of food production fostered economic and professional specialization; as we go from bands to states, there are more possible roles that people can fill by virtue of the fact that fewer people can produce enough to sustain greater numbers.

Again, as is appreciated now, such a model is not progressive; societies are not naturally developing *toward* inherently better industrial states and there are many pathways to societal change. There have been many cases of massive state-level societies breaking down into agglomerations of small-scale societies (e.g., the Maya) or complex chiefdom societies from previously horticultural-hunting contexts that became subsistence hunters when introduced to new contexts (e.g., Siouan groups dominating the American Great Plains and adopting bison-hunting).

Service's scheme continues to be useful; while crude and can still tempt us to think progressively, this model nonetheless helps generate new inferences about a wide range of cultural traits, particularly when coupled with other theoretical frames and observations (for a more contemporary view, see Kaplan, Hooper, & Gurven, 2009). If we know how a society procured food, for example, we can make reasonable predictions about its predominant form of political decision-making. Bands, for example, are typically egalitarian and make decisions collectively (Boehm, 1993) whereas states tend to make decisions in a top-down fashion. Furthermore, the model offers a mechanism – food production – as an important driver of societal change. In other words, if we know something about how a society makes a living, we can predict a lot about cultural forms, including aspects of religion.

Take, for instance, how anthropologist A. R. Wallace (1966) built upon this general scheme. While he did not explicitly appeal to Service's model, Wallace's typology of religions certainly corresponds to it (see Table 1). Here, the content and structures of religion and society co-evolve; egalitarian bands with a more equitable distribution of decision-making power also tend to have shamanic traditions where spirits are distributed throughout the landscape. In contrast, the structures of chiefdoms correspond to structures of polytheism where important figureheads are "at the top" with increasing numbers of those with less influence are "at the bottom." According to the model, states – societies with hyper-concentrations of power – trend toward having monotheistic high gods with supreme power. Like we saw with Tylor and Durkheim, Wallace's model really suggests that these religious types are reflections of how a society is structured.

Regarding the relationship between morality and religion, Wallace's view is in keeping with the anthropological wisdom of the time, asserting that "In every society there is a sacred oral or written literature which asserts what is truth in religion. This code...contains the *moral injunctions* of prophets and of gods" (57). Thus, the moral dictates of the gods are central to all religious traditions. Further, he notes that "Contrary to some popular impressions and to Tylor's early summary of observations (1871a, 1871b), even the most primitive peoples often regard violation of the moral code as entailing the threat of supernatural punishment," qualifying that "Supernatural sanctions for morality are more likely to be invoked in societies where there are, between persons, considerable social differences derived from differences in wealth" (193). Unlike his predecessors, Wallace could appeal to cross-cultural, *quantitative* data. Citing a landmark achievement, namely, sociologist Guy Swanson's (1964) cross-cultural study, *The Birth of the Gods*, Wallace effectively united the anthropology of religion with a revolution in cross-cultural inquiry.

3.2 The Birth of Cross-Cultural Datasets

As the Service-Wallace model suggests, once worldwide observations of other, non-European populations became more commonplace, patterns in the beliefs, practices, and other cultural traits became easier to make. However, while Service and Wallace's models are useful, how reliable are they? How representative are they of the populations they claim to describe? How reliable and robust are the relationships we think are out there? As noted earlier, it is easy enough to cherry-pick examples and counter-examples to support or refute a specific argument. It is another task entirely to systematically and reliably assess whether a pattern exists.

Because of the uncertainty and informality associated with single-shot qualitative observations, social scientists increasingly embraced the used of quantitative data and its analysis (Murdock & White, 1969). Interestingly, this demand led to the compilation and development of cross-cultural repositories and databases of materials about far-flung populations. Central to their process was the quantification of previous generations' qualitative reports.

As it turns out, one of the first – if not *the* first – quantitative cross-cultural databases was devoted to understanding the relationship between religion and society (for what may be the first cross-cultural database using categorical codes, see Murdock, 1957). Swanson's *The Birth of the Gods* (1964) represents a remarkable step forward in the social sciences.

Swanson and his two assistants scoured ethnographic materials from fifty diverse societies from around the world (32–37). Focusing on a host of variables ranging from whether societies had debt and social classes to supernatural sanctions for morality and beliefs in magic, this small team converted qualitative ethnographic observations into quantitative data (e.g., *Is reincarnation present?*; 0 = absent; 1 = present – in human form; 2 = present – in animal form).[9] The book then applies a variety of statistical tests to assess various hypotheses of interest.

Swanson's dataset – and others like it – is really about the *available and/or sampled ethnographic record*, not necessarily the ethnographic reality behind it. We'll revisit this point later, but it helps to remind ourselves how some information might be lost, ignored, or created by virtue of the production of ethnographic materials and its subsequent quantification (Cronk, 1998; Watts et al., 2022). What happens when an ethnographer doesn't mention a particular trait? In Swanson's view, we might treat the absence of evidence as evidence of absence for two reasons (51). First, he assumes that Western ethnographers would be likely to report, for example, a "high, monotheistic god" because such gods are similar to their own cultural backgrounds. Second, he assumes that ethnographers would only bother to document the *absence* of a trait only when that absence is surprising or notable in some important way. He recognizes that maintaining this set of assumptions "will undoubtedly lead us into some errors," though the severity and prevalence of such errors are left unaddressed. Swanson ultimately appeals to the utility of the assumption on the grounds that a proper study needs data, that is, "we need as many judgements about as many of the societies in our sample as possible" (51–52). So, there might be some errors by adopting these assumptions, but to him, the benefits of doing a study with more data outweigh the costs of introducing errors in that data.

---

[9] In terms of scientific transparency and reproducibility, this little volume was way ahead of its time. Not only does it include the entire data set, but it also provides: (a) definitions for its 39 variables, (b) citations of the specific ethnographic source materials Swanson and his team coded, and (c) the general rules they followed to code the data.

To his credit, Swanson makes these assumptions explicit. But how safe are they? We might just as easily assume the converse idea that ethnographers would not bother reporting things that are common or well understood by their anthropological peers. Considering the ethnographer's primary job is to document and account for human variation, they might naturally emphasise the differences found in the societies they study rather than the similarities, even if they are present (Naroll & Naroll, 1963). Furthermore, it might be the case that some topics are ignored because of more salient activities. So, for example, beliefs in a "high god" might be present in a society, but they might have been ignored because, say, ancestor spirits were more often discussed in daily activities and ritual activities were more notable. We'll return to this issue later. Keeping these issues in mind, let us first examine Swanson's theoretical motivations behind the topic at hand.

In the chapter "The Supernatural and Morality," Swanson briefly surveys the intellectual history of the topic, suggesting that "The people of modern Western nations are so steeped in these beliefs which bind religion and morality, that they find it hard to conceive of societies which separate the two" (153). He proceeds to discuss Tylor's, Malinowski's, and other influential thinkers' views on the subject (see Section 2), concluding that "We can be certain that Tylor's view is not universally valid for primitive societies, but that it does fit some of them" (155). Swanson suggests that much of the disagreement between Tylor and Malinowski are to be found in their unclear and inconsistent use of "morality."

Unfortunately, Swanson does not help us much in the effort to clarify what "morality" refers to. In summarizing the differences between Tylor's and Malinowski's views, he rests on the following: "Morals are social rules which specify the behaviours required of those who enter moral relationships and seek to maintain them" (156) and "a moral relationship exists to the extent that self-conscious beings intentionally and freely facilitate the achievement of one another's goals and intentionally and freely accept this facilitation from each other" (157). So, "moral relationships" are partnerships that allow the involved parties to achieve each other's goals. "Moral rules" are the guidelines that must be followed to facilitate the moral relationships. It is anything one *ought* to do when helping others achieve their desires. Thus, this particular definition allows just about anything interpersonal to fall under the aegis of "moral" (e.g., sitting in one's seat in a classroom would thus be a "moral" issue with respect to facilitating a teacher's job).

Drawing from this, he concludes that "It would be strange indeed if the deities which represent sovereign groups were totally indifferent to actions which violate the bonds of loyalty that bind members to those groups" (159) and while "the ethnographic evidence supports the judgment that moral relations between particular individuals are not always subjected to supernatural sanctions...in some respects, the supernatural is frequently involved in supporting human morality" (ibid.). Thus, there remains variation to be explained. In his quest to understand this variation, Swanson offers three theoretical predictions:

- "Any important but unstable moral relationship between individuals...will evoke supernatural sanctions to buttress their fragile association" (159)
- "Supernatural controls cannot be exercised over interpersonal relations unless the number of persons having interests peculiar to themselves has become great enough to create a large number of social relations in which people interact as particular individuals, rather than as members of some group" (160)
- "Supernatural controls are exercised over interpersonal relations in all societies, but this belief becomes explicit only when the conditions cited under the first hypothesis force people to become aware of the facts" (160).

In terms of theory, while these three hypotheses all have functional implications inasmuch as they suggest that appeals to supernatural punishment can have an effect, Swanson stresses the conditions under which gods and other spiritual agents (e.g., *karma* or *mana*) will be explicitly associated with moral relationships: (a) when moral relationships are important and delicate; (b) when there are considerable competing interests among individuals to manage; and (c) when people are aware of how important and delicate their moral relationships are. The third hypothesis is notable for a few reasons. First, it declares that *all societies exhibit supernatural controls over interpersonal relations*. Second, it brings hypotheses to a measurable, almost psychological level by identifying the conditions under which religion becomes *explicitly* – rather than tacitly – about morality. We will revisit this distinction between religion's implicit and explicit moral relevance in the next section.

Swanson admits that he can't directly test these hypotheses using his data. Instead, he operationalizes (i.e., converts concepts into measurable units) moralistic supernatural sanctions by examining the reported presence of supernatural sanctions across indices of things that might threaten moral relationships such as "debt relations, social classes, [and] individually owned property" (162). This is a curiously narrow subset of the moral domain! He also admits that one of the more sizeable problems with coding this data is

> the absence of direct evidence that particular relationships between people meet our criteria of morality or that the persons concerned are interacting as particular individuals rather than as members of a group. All one can say is that the records contain those instances in which *sanctions of supernatural origin are applied to persons because these persons help or harm other members of the same society*. (163–164, emphasis added)

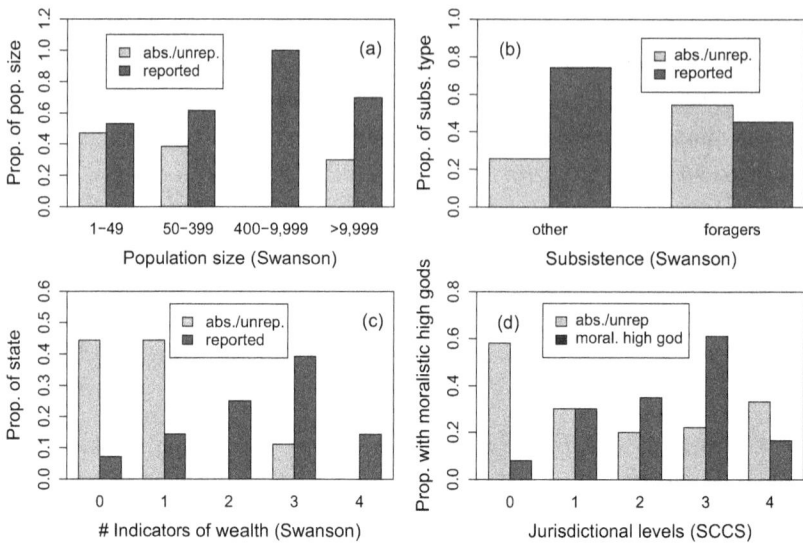

Figure 1 Barplot of distribution of supernatural sanctions for morality across (a) population sizes, (b) foraging, and (c) indicators of wealth in Swanson's data set. Panel (d) is the distribution of absent or unreported "high" gods and reported moralistic high gods across number of jurisdictional levels (i.e., column proportions from Table 2; missing values not considered) in the SCCS.

In this admission, "moral" now means "help or harm," thus offering something a little more concrete and precise in the way of what "moral" means that he offered earlier. In terms of method, Swanson once again points to the gulf between ethnographic reality, theoretical constructs, their operationalization, and the source material used to create data. Given these sizable caveats, what do the data show?

According to Swanson's data, 67% of the groups have sampled records mentioning supernatural sanctions for behaviors that "help or harm other members of the same society" (33/49 as one's population size was uncertain). That means that only sixteen societies' records lacked mention or reported the absence of supernatural sanctions for morality. Figure 1a shows this across population sizes. If we take Service's model seriously, even among those smallest of societies with populations under fifty people (likely foragers), there are roughly as many with (53%) moralistic supernatural sanctions as those without (47%). In other words, *half of the smallest societies were reported to have moralistic supernatural punishment*. Furthermore, it is clear that the presence of supernatural sanctions for morality is at least at this level across population sizes. Figure 1b shows that roughly half (45%) of all societies whose principal source of food is collecting and gathering, fishing, or hunting have reported instance of moralistic supernatural punishment.

Swanson also assessed the relationship between the number of indicators of wealth disparities and the presence of supernatural sanctions for "help or harm [toward] other members of the same society" (164; Figure 1c). Out of the fifty societies studied, only thirty-seven had "pertinent data" (168).[10] While the numbers are low, 76% of this truncated sample have records indicating the presence of supernatural sanctions, suggesting that "these sanctions are widespread in our sample" (168). After conducting a multitude of tests, Swanson concludes that, "Contrary to Tylor's formulation, *a considerable proportion of the simpler peoples do make a connection between supernatural sanctions and moral behavior*" (174, emphasis added).

In terms of accounting for the variation in types of beliefs, moralistic "sanctions are more likely to appear in societies in which there are interpersonal differences according to wealth" (174). The most generous we can be about this particular finding is that there is a correlation; we do not know what causes what (for critique, see Peregrine, 1996). Do such beliefs develop in response to the accumulation of wealth? Do they function to reduce inequality? Or do such beliefs curb self-indulgence? These two traits – moralistic supernatural sanctions and wealth disparities – could also co-evolve. As we'll see, subsequent efforts have tried to address these questions more rigorously.

Swanson's text also includes a chapter dedicated to monotheism, which he defines "as the first cause of all effects and the necessary and sufficient condition for reality's continued existence" (55). Here, Swanson also defines "high gods" as creator deities that are "ultimately responsible for all events, whether as history's creator, its director, or both" (56). Merging these two criteria into a single "high gods" construct, Swanson finds that the presence of such gods tends to be associated with societies with more sovereign, hierarchically structured organization and those with more than a single sovereign communal group (Figure 1d). This resonates with the Service-Wallace model; hierarchical societies with bureaucracies have gods that resemble chairmen. While these aspects of social complexity indicate the presence of high gods, others, such as occupational specialization, are less clear. As it turns out, Swanson's high gods variable contributed to resources that spawned decades of cross-cultural research. Unfortunately, due to the heavy reliance on "high gods," this research lost sight of the global ubiquity of moralistic supernatural sanctions that had been appreciated for generations and tested and confirmed by Swanson's important contribution.

---

[10] It's curious that in this case, Swanson does not equate absence of evidence with evidence of absence.

3.3 High Gods, Morality, and Social Complexity

With Swanson's help, anthropologists Murdock and White developed the Standard Cross-Cultural Sample (SCCS), a cross-cultural database of many variables regarding 186 different societies. The SCCS is a calculated subsample of the more encompassing Ethnographic Atlas (EA, Murdock, 1967). Murdock and White designed this subsample specifically to avoid what is known as "Galton's Problem" (Naroll, 1961, 1965).

In response to a lecture by E. B. Tylor (1889), Francis Galton raised the issue that when trying to functionally explain the cross-cultural presence of certain traditions, one must be sure to attend to the possibility that cultural parentage or borrowing might explain why two or more populations share the target trait. Having a massive number of populations in a database – some of which are interacting with each other, were historically the same group, or are learning traits from a common source (e.g., colonial powers or missionaries) – might muddy any analyses that presume cultural independence.

Like Swanson's data, the EA and SCCS consist of quantitative data derived from qualitative reports. Unlike Swanson's data, however, both draw from a wider range of source types beyond ethnography, including reports from missionaries and travelers and holy books (e.g., the Bible is one source for the Hebrews).[11] Furthermore, while the data in *The Birth of the Gods* were largely devoted to religious data, the EA and SCCS have only a few variables pertaining to religion and only one variable that addresses gods' association with morality.

Coming directly from Swanson (1964), the "high god" variable (V34 and V238 of the EA and SCCS respectively) indicates the presence of various states of having a "high god" as recorded and coded in the records from which the EA and SCCS drew. According to these sources, a "high god" is: "a spiritual being who is believed to have created all reality and/or to be its ultimate governor, even though his/her sole act was to create other spirits who, in turn, created or control the natural world" (Swanson, 1964, 210). In addition to "data unavailable" (see Dow and Eff, 2009 for discussion of missing data in the SCCS), there are four categorical options as possible values for high gods:

0. absent or not reported [in the materials]
1. present but not active in human affairs
2. present and active in human affairs but not supportive of human morality
3. present, active, and specifically supportive of human morality

---

[11] The qualitative texts from which these datasets are derived are stored in the Human Area Relations Files repository (Ember, 2007). Revised versions of the EA and SCCS can be obtained at D-PLACE, a database repository, https://d-place.org/.

Table 2 Frequencies of high god code types across levels of jurisdictional hierarchy levels from SCCS. High god code types correspond to categories detailed earlier. NA refers to "data unavailable." Row proportions do not include NA values.

	0	1	2	3	4	NA
abs./unreported	43 (63%)	13 (19%)	4 (6%)	4 (6%)	4 (6%)	0
inactive	17 (36%)	15 (32%)	6 (13%)	3 (6%)	6 (13%)	0
active, nonmoral	8 (62%)	2 (15%)	3 (23%)	0 (0%)	0 (0%)	0
active, moral	6 (15%)	13 (33%)	7 (18%)	11 (28%)	2 (5%)	1
NA	8	5	3	1	0	1

Recall the earlier issue regarding the absence of evidence Swanson raised. Since these are data coded from qualitative materials – and we know a little about the quality of such records (Section 2) – we might adopt a little more caution and maintain that just because a trait is not reported doesn't mean it should be considered absent. The authors of some sources might have overlooked a trait, perhaps they didn't ask, or perhaps they had their own agendas. In fact, the sources characterizing the Abipón Indians as "slow, dull and stupid" were among those that led to the coding of their high gods as "absent or not reported" in the EA and SCCS! Oddly, this coding scheme explicitly conflates the options of "absent" and "not reported" and without looking at the source material, we wouldn't know why the data wound up being coded this way. Even when we do, the answers are not immediately forthcoming.

Furthermore, as previous generations would anticipate, there are numerous cases of gods and spirits that are clearly associated with morality that aren't specifically high gods. Consider the traditionally horticulturalist Orokaiva of Papua New Guinea and the foraging Ainu of Japan. Both societies are coded as having "absent or unreported" high gods. The former are coded as having one level of jurisdictional hierarchy, while the latter are coded as having two. Yet, the literature used to code these values reveals an explicit association between traditional gods and morality:

> If the Orokaiva, by and large, order their lives by the same moral principles, they would explain this by their common belief in certain demigods whom they all regard as their ancestors and as sources of authority, and who created certain institutions embodying moral norms to which they all subscribe. Not only do they obey the precepts of these demi-gods, they also re-enact their feats in ritual and identify with them during ceremonies, and in many of their regular expressive activities (Schwimmer, 1973, 51).

> The power of the deities is demonstrated to the Ainu not only through their beneficial power in providing abundant food and general welfare but also through their power to punish by causing an illness if offended ...The ultimate cause of these illnesses lies with humans, who can please these beings so that they remain beneficial or benign or break a taboo and bring about their own misfortune. Thus, an illness is incurred by breaking moral codes against deities or other soul-bearing beings of the universe, or by breaking social codes against fellow Ainu with the use of offensive remarks (Ohnuki-Tierney, 1981, 80).

So, even if these traditions lack high gods, they do include gods that are unambiguously associated with morality. As such, if our interest lies in the relationship between morality and the gods, relying on the high gods variable will mislead.

With these words of caution in mind, what do the data tell us? Table 2 reports the raw data across different levels of "jurisdictional hierarchy," a variable often used to denote social complexity. Just by eyeballing these data, we can see that over half of the societies in the SCCS have one level of jurisdictional hierarchy or less. Sixty-eight (37%) societies were coded with "absent or not reported" high gods with nearly a quarter (43) of the entire sample were societies lacking high gods *and* had no levels of jurisdictional hierarchy. In terms of the distribution of moralistic high gods in the sample, there really isn't much of a pattern to see across jurisdictional hierarchy (see Figure 1d). The proportion of moralistic high gods present increases slightly as we increase jurisdictional levels, but drops again at the highest level of societal complexity.

Many studies have exploited this variable in the EA and SCCS data sets (see Table 3). Notably, while each report offers a novel spin on the subject, all find that social complexity and/or its correlates predict moralistic high gods. Some find that subsistence predicts the presence of high gods (e.g., Simpson, 1984; Underhill, 1975), but given the concentration of "absent/not reported" values among societies with no levels of jurisdictional hierarchy (presumably foragers), this should be unsurprising.

In one article, Snarey (1996) looks beyond social complexity and mode of subsistence and assesses the relationship between water scarcity and the presence of high gods "specifically supportive of human morality." Snarey's hypothesis is stated as follows: "In societies in which ensuring a sufficient supply of water is difficult, the members of that society will be significantly more likely to conceive of a Supreme Deity who is concerned with, and supportive of, human morality"' (88). While the prediction is relatively clear, the reason why "Supreme Deities" – rather than *any* type of morally concerned deity – matter here is not explained. So, the relationship between morality, the gods,

Table 3 Resources and empirical works on the topic of morality and the gods including cross-cultural data or data from non-Western societies. Sources are as follows: EA – Ethnographic Atlas; SCCS – Standard Cross-Cultural Sample; AWC – Atlas of World Cultures; WVS – World Values Survey; DRH – Database of Religious History; ERM – Evolution of Religion and Morality Project

Source	Data
Swanson (1964)	coded data
Murdock (1967)	EA
Murdock & White (1969)	SCCS
Simpson (1984)	SCCS
J. P. Gray (1987)	SCCS
Peregrine (1996)	coded data
Snarey (1996)	SCCS
Stark (2001)	AWC, WVS
Roes & Raymond (2003)	EA, SCCS
D. D. P. Johnson (2005)	SCCS
Boehm (2008)	coded data
Sanderson and Roberts (2008)	SCCS
C. Brown & Eff (2010)	SCCS
Atkinson & Bourrat (2011)	WVS
Bourrat, Atkinson, & Dunbar (2011)	SCCS
Purzycki (2011)	quant. ethnographic
Peoples & Marlowe (2012)	SCCS
Purzycki (2013a)	quant. ethnographic
Botero et al. (2014)	EA
Roes (2014)	EA, SCCS
Baumard, et al. (2015)	coded data
Turchin et al. (2015)	SESHAT
Watts, Greenhill, et al. (2015)	Pulotu
Watts, Sheehan, et al. (2015)	Pulotu
Peoples, Duda, & Marlowe (2016)	SCCS
Purzycki et al. (2016)	ERM
Ge, Chen, Wu, & Mace (2019)	experimental
M. Lang et al. (2019)	ERM
Whitehouse et al. (2019 [RETRACTED])	SESHAT
Jackson, et al (2020)	SCCS
Skoggard, et al. (2020)	SCCS

Table 3 (Cont.)

Source	Data
Townsend, et al. (2020)	quant. ethnographic
Ember, et al. (2021)	SCCS
Singh, et al. (2021)	quant. ethnographic
Danielson et al. (2022)	DRH
Purzycki, Willard, et al. (2022)	ERM
Turchin et al. (2023b)	SESHAT
Bentzen & Gokmen (2022)	EA, SCCS
Bendixen et al. (2023)	ERM

and water scarcity is actually measured in terms of high gods. Snarey found evidence consistent with his hypothesis.

Nearly a decade later, Roes and Raymond (2003) used the EA and SCCS to assess the relationship between population size, external conflict, and religion. Drawing from evolutionary biologist Richard D. Alexander's theory of morality (1987, see below) that holds that intergroup conflict over resources boosts population size, the authors wager that one mechanism to hold such large populations together are beliefs in "moralizing gods." Specifically, "Belief in these gods signals acceptance of the rules and…we expect more support for the rules (and thus more belief in moralising gods) in larger societies" (128). Using jurisdictional hierarchy as an index of society size, the authors indeed find a positive relationship between society size and the presence of moralizing *high* gods. Like Snarey, the authors make no clear justification for why moralizing *high gods* would matter more or less than *any* moralizing god. Thus, we see the recurrence of the conflation of moralizing gods with moralizing *high* gods. As we'll see, this conflation has had a lasting impact on contemporary inquiry.

In summary, quantitative cross-cultural databases arose as a response to a need for tools to examine global patterns of cultural variation. This resource was specifically developed to address questions of *religious* variation, and it found that supernatural involvement in moral affairs was commonplace in the ethnographic world. Subsequent, more expansive databases primarily limited their focus to high gods, of which many studies had taken advantage, finding again and again a positive association between social complexity and high gods that were "specifically supportive of human morality." Despite this narrow focus on high gods, its troubling coding scheme, at least some dubious source material, the repeated exploitation of these cross-cultural databases eclipsed generations of dedicated inquiry.

Many of the later group-level reports using cross-cultural databases came out at a time of increased interest in the evolutionary psychological foundations of religion. Rather than focusing on coarse, group-level phenomena coded from various texts, evolutionary research emphasized individual cognition and behavior in experimental and field contexts. As we'll see, this new focus also generated new and more precise ways of thinking about and measuring the relationship between morality and the gods.

4 Cognition and Religion
4.1 Genesis of New Fields
4.1.1 Cognitive Science

While the division has existed in various guises for centuries, in the 1980s and 1990s, some sectors of the social sciences witnessed a widening gulf between those who embraced various forms of nativism (i.e., a position that emphasizes innate cognitive systems) and those who emphasized cultural learning as the ultimate explanation for human behavior.[12] Drawing from the ideas of linguist Noam Chomsky and philosopher Jerry Fodor, who pointed to innate cognitive systems to account for much of human thought and language, many social scientists began to propose a wide range of inborn cognitive mechanisms underlying other domains of culture. Much of this literature alludes to what is called the "poverty of the stimulus argument" which points to just how much *isn't* taught that children nevertheless express (Chomsky, 1965). For example, children don't have to be taught what language is or that objects fall when they reach the edge of a table or that solid objects can't pass through each other. Rather, they *infer* what language is, they *infer* that an object will fall, and they *infer* that solid objects will collide. Similarly, the grammar of a language emerges from deeper structures and knowledge of syntax that the child already has. According to some views, such inferences are made possible by virtue of innate cognitive systems.

Some theories specified particular features that defined these cognitive systems. Sometimes referred to as cognitive "modules," these mental instincts were thought to be innate, handle a narrow range of inputs, and relatively automatic in their functioning (Fodor, 1983). Some held that the mind was only minimally modular in this sense, where modules were restricted to perhaps emotional responses, the perception of optical illusions, and some aspects of human language. Others took this view further and, in relaxing some of the

---
[12] This section draws from Purzycki, Pisor, et al. (2018) and Purzycki and Willard (2016).

criteria for what counts as a "module," suggested that the mind is replete with modular structures that underlie a wide range of human traits (e.g., Pinker, 1997; Sperber, 1996).

4.1.2 Evolutionary psychology

Alongside a well-organized critique of the "standard social science model" – the view that most human behavior is socially learned and that the mind is effectively an all-purpose *tabula rasa* (i.e., blank slate) – researchers deduced the presence of a wide range of modules, including those dedicated to numbers, music, spatial cognition, and many others (Barkow, Cosmides, & Tooby, 1995; Hirschfeld & Gelman, 1994). Some took this view even further and theorized that many such mechanisms evolved by way of natural selection; these modules were advantageous for our ancestors to have and this explains their universality and often context-specific functioning. Among others, these commitments were core to the nascent state of "evolutionary psychology."

This field heavily influenced major theories of culture as well. In one approach, culture was made possible – and more likely to be a part of a group's repertoire – because of these evolved cognitive structures. With the suggestion that evolved cognition functioned to generate intuitive inferences about our world and these mechanisms have the capacity to attract corresponding cultural information, theory increasingly minimized the significance of learning and trial-and-error in accounting for human thought and behavior.

Some drew from this increased interest in instinct to develop models of human cognition. Popular "dual-process" models made the distinction between "fast" intuitive cognition on the one hand, and "slow," more deliberate reasoning on the other (see Kahneman, 2003). Building on this, other models made the distinction between *intuitive* and *reflective* beliefs (see Sperber, 1996, 1997). Here, "beliefs" refer to any general mental idea or inference about our world that one might hold to be at least partly true. Roughly speaking, intuitive beliefs are rapidly produced and the source of or process behind producing such beliefs is not a part of one's experience of the belief. For example, we might quickly infer that because the ground is wet and the sky is dark and cloudy, it has recently rained. We are not likely aware of the process behind that inference (e.g., logic, the structure of the syllogism of the inference, the recall of previous experience, etc.).

Intuitive beliefs are often conflated with beliefs that emerge from evolved cognition. As philosopher Dan Sperber (1996) notes: "Intuitive beliefs owe their rationality to essentially innate, hence universal, perceptual and inferential mechanisms; as a result, they do not vary dramatically, and are essentially mutually consistent or reconcilable across cultures" (91–92). Reflective beliefs, on the other hand, are more effortful and the process by which we arrive at them is very much a deliberate, conscious process. So, dividing 600 by 12.98 requires some effort and the means we arrive at our belief in the answer is the process of division. Thinking through one's top ten favorite songs takes some reflection as the reasons why certain songs appear is a conscious part of the process. Of course, if we relax the association between "intuitive beliefs' rationality" and "innate", there is an intuitive-reflective continuum and one person's reflective beliefs might be perfectly intuitive for someone else. As we'll see, the cognitive science of religion crystallized these ideas and applied them in various ways to religious phenomena.

4.1.3 Cognitive Science of Religion

The cognitive science of religion grew directly out of evolutionary psychological thinking. While no one suggested we have a "religion" or "god" module, many argued that the cognitive foundations of religion stemmed from evolved and/or innate cognitive systems. Much of the early thinking in the cognitive science of religion endorsed the view that religious phenomena were largely by-products of our evolved minds (Atran, 2004; Barrett, 2004; Boyer, 2007). Linguist Steven Pinker sums up this view nicely: "[humans] enjoy strawberry cheesecake, but not because we evolved a taste for it. We evolved circuits that gave us trickles of enjoyment from the sweet taste of ripe fruit, the creamy mouth feel of fats and oils from nuts and meat, and the coolness of fresh water" (Pinker, 1997, 524–525). In other words, humans have things like religion, music, and art because they have elements of things that had past value that we evolved to appreciate, but they remain attractive because they trigger these ancestral traits. Such things are found everywhere because of their intuitive appeal. This view treats cultural information like an epidemic; cultural things like music and literature spread like diseases because our innate cognition attracts them.

In the context of religion, these cognitive systems provide *intuitive* information that attracts beliefs and practices. For example, some examine whether intuitive mind-body dualism underlies beliefs in spirits (Chudek et al., 2018). Others treat ritual as having its own "grammar" with corresponding cognitive foundations (Lawson & McCauley, 1993) while others argue that the punctiliousness we so often exhibit with ritual stems from evolved "hazard precaution systems" (Liénard & Boyer, 2006). Researchers have pointed to a variety of other cognitive foundations of religion, all united in suggesting that the curious elements associated with religion we find around the world emerge from the way our minds naturally work (C. White, 2021).

One important set of religious beliefs comes from our ability to infer that other beings have mental states – beliefs, desires, and perceptions. While other species likely have this ability to some degree, humans' mentalizing abilities are notably complex and nuanced (Call & Tomasello, 2008; D. C. Penn & Povinelli, 2007). This "mindreading system" consists of a variety of sub-mechanisms ostensibly shaped by natural selection that animate the entities of our world with mental states (Baron-Cohen, 1997). One particularly influential idea is that among the central cognitive foundations of religion are our anthropomorphic or "mentalizing" tendencies; we are so good at detecting mental states and granting nonhumans the ability to symbolically communicate.

In this view, religious cognition is this trait in action. Building upon centuries of thought, anthropologist Stewart Guthrie (1980, 1995) argued that our rapid perceptual biases toward detecting other minds accounts for our religiosity. In doing so, Guthrie grounded elements of Tylor's theory of animism in human cognition (cf. Guthrie, 2000). Guthrie added an evolutionary spin to his argument, suggesting that our ancestors – and other animals more generally – survived in the past because it was always better to detect another agent's threat when there wasn't one (i.e., a false positive) than it was to *not* detect a threat when there was one (i.e., a false negative). Individuals were more likely to survive when they erred on the side of caution. As such, it is effortless for us to find minds in the natural world. Psychologist Justin Barrett (2004) pursued this idea, postulating the presence of a "hyperactive agency detection" system that detected minds with just a few of the right kinds of inputs. This device makes conveying the idea of a spirit or god – an anthropomorphic mind with unique properties – especially easy to learn and internalize. In order to believe that gods or spirits care about us, we must be able to infer that they have minds in the first place. Such inferences are fast, intuitive, and come to us naturally.

What about reflective and/or cultural beliefs? Surely religious beliefs and practices are more than what come naturally to our minds. The specifics of some beliefs are obviously cultural; from the Crucifixion to sacred garden groves, many central beliefs are culturally transmitted across the generations. Yet, some are bafflingly complicated and require generations of theologians to offer solutions. The indivisibility of the Trinity and the Problem of Evil, for example, are nontrivial problems on which theologians have expended considerable effort. Some of the founders of the cognitive science of religion point to a distinction between reflective and intuitive beliefs as useful to account for kinds of religious thought and practice, suggesting that much of religious expression stems from our intuitions (Slone, 2007). We might have long, drawn out theological discussions about the nature of spirits and the universe, and these are deliberate reflective thoughts. However, the idea that a god knows things or the inference that a drum makes a louder sound when hit harder are both perfectly intuitive thoughts. What's interesting about religious cognition is that sometimes our intuitions are inconsistent with our reflections; our own minds often get in the way of what we're supposed to believe about the minds of gods.

One set of experiments (Barrett & Keil, 1996) showed that even though individuals claim that the Christian god knows and perceives everything, after reading a passage that describes some event, participants readily limit his ability as though he were a human. For example, participants read one scenario where God is admiring a colorful rock, but then a stampede runs by and covers it with dust. When recalling the story, individuals – who claim God perceives everything – suggest that God's vision of the rock was obscured by the dust. What this inconsistency suggests is that people are using their intuitive beliefs about *people* – beings with limited perceptual abilities – to quickly make sense of a scenario *even though* they claim that the agent involved is omniscient; an all-knowing entity should still be able to see and appreciate the stone after it was covered with dust. Had individuals been using their more abstract theological statements when perceiving the story, they would have said as much. As we'll see, this interplay between explicit religious beliefs and how individuals intuitively think in real-time plays a role in making sense of the relationship between morality and the gods. In order to appreciate these developments, we need to first briefly review the evolutionary psychology of morality.

4.2 Cognitive Foundations of Religion and Morality

4.2.1 Evolutionary Psychology of Morality

As we've already seen hints of, the subject of morality has had a long and diverse history (Malle & Robbins, 2025). As in any other field striving to understand elusive, multifaceted theoretical constructs, various researchers tend to emphasize different things. In keeping with philosopher Immanuel Kant's (1997 [1785]) categorical imperative, some appeal to universal applicability; morality involves prescriptive behaviors that are applicable to *everyone* at all times (Caton, 1963). Such views attend to the *scope* of moral relevance. Others focus on the *content* of what counts as "moral." For example, developmental psychologist Eliot Turiel (1983, 2006) famously considers morality as things concerning "justice, rights, and welfare." However, the content and scope of what counts as moral is known to vary cross-culturally, and groups often lack abstract notions like "justice" and "rights," or don't specify or limit whom and to what situations moral prescriptions apply (Fessler et al., 2015; Schwartz, 2007; Shweder et al., 1997). Indeed, the difficulty in precisely delimiting what constitutes morality is only exacerbated by Western-centric approaches to the topic. As cultural and evolutionary anthropologist Christopher Boehm (1980) mused, "when the subject is morality, possibilities for ethnocentric, personal, and theoretical biases of the ethnographer to distort indigenous 'psychological realities' are maximal" (3). However, there does appear to be an emerging consensus in the field.

Part of that consensus lies in the relationship between our mentalizing abilities and their relevance to morality. Many have examined the strong psychological link between mind perception and moral cognition (K. Gray, Young, & Waytz 2012; Imuta et al. 2016; Young & Phillips 2011). In particular, perspective-taking is essential to engage in "good" behavior and avoid "bad" behavior; this kind of empathizing is necessary for strong, stable relationships. So, when we use our mentalizing abilities, we engage our moral sensibilities by default.

Another part of that consensus lies in morality's function. Though diverse (e.g., Cronk, 1994; Machery & Mallon, 2010), evolutionary accounts of morality have long considered the psychology underlying beliefs and behaviors that approximate the "moral," with the premise that these beliefs and behaviors generate individual- and/or group-level benefits. In a statement that presaged the aforementioned distinction between evolved capacities, social learning, and reason, Charles Darwin (1871) focused on the relationship between "social instincts" in humans and the ontogeny (i.e., individual development) of reciprocity, suggesting that "the social instincts...with the aid of active intellectual powers and the effects of habit, naturally lead to the golden rule...and this lies at the foundation of morality" (151). Here, Darwin elegantly ties together biology, acculturation, and reason to account for models of how to treat others. Building on this general framing, biologist Richard Alexander (1987) suggests that "*immoral* is a label we apply to...acts by which we help ourselves or hurt others, while acts that hurt ourselves or help others are more likely to be judged moral than immoral," noting that "it is not easy to be more precise in defining" the domain (12). In sum, these views suggest that the *content* of morality boils down to how we treat others, and the *scope* of morality pertains to how individuals treat others.

Evolutionary psychological approaches to morality build upon this general framework, but also have their own idiosyncratic conceptions of the content and scope of the moral domain (see Cosmides & Tooby, 2005). For example, while some emphasize psychological adaptations that mitigate problems in cooperation and coordination (Greene, 2013), others offer broader purviews of "moral systems" defined as "interlocking sets of values, virtues, norms, practices, identities, institutions, technologies, and evolved psychological mechanisms that work together to suppress or regulate selfishness and make cooperative social life possible" (Haidt & Kesebir, 2010, 800). Of course, many evolutionary thinkers emphasize morality's *function* in promoting cooperation. For instance, Tomasello and Vaish (2013) argue that morality's "main function...is to regulate an individual's social interactions with others in the general direction of cooperation, given that all individuals are at least somewhat selfish" (232). Despite diversity in conceptualizations, evolutionary psychological approaches agree that human reciprocity and cooperation are a manifestation of morality's evolutionary heritage. A considerable bulk of the remaining efforts revolve around problems pertaining to the content and scope of evolved morality.

One content problem largely consists of what the evolved domains of morality actually are (for review, see K. Gray & Pratt, 2025). Take, for example, the popular "Moral Foundations" literature. Seeking to better operationalize the moral domain with attention to cross-cultural validity, this work breaks down the evolutionary psychological "foundations" of morality into a few core dimensions (i.e., dedicated and distinct cognitive systems that handle specific aspects of morality). While the rubric itself has evolved (Graham et al., 2013), the most recent iteration includes: (1) harm/care; (2) fairness/reciprocity; (3) ingroup/loyalty; (4) authority/respect, and (5) purity/sanctity as foundational to moral reasoning. In contrast, the more recent "Morality-as-Cooperation" literature (Curry, 2016; Curry, Chesters, & Van Lissa, 2019) measures seven types of cooperation treated as the foundations of moral behavior: (1) family values; (2) group loyalty; (3) reciprocity; (4) dominance; (5) deference; (6) fairness; and (7) rights to property. These categories reflect sub-domains of moral reasoning and the salient values that people might hold cross-culturally. Both approaches adopt the stance that moral systems are fundamentally about cooperation. Evidence from coded cross-cultural materials shows that around the world, people certainly treat aspects of cooperation as "good" (Curry, Mullins, & Whitehouse, 2019). Yet, when individuals list what it means to be good and bad, it can be difficult to classify the things they list using these rubrics (e.g., is "honesty" about fairness or deference? is "kindness" about group loyalty or reciprocity? see Purzycki, Pisor, et al., 2018). Nevertheless, such items are easily nestled in the greater context of cooperation.

So far, we've pointed to the evolutionary psychological literature that investigates the purported biological foundations of the moral domain. While varying, the literature addressing the content problem of the moral domain ultimately addresses what individuals and communities think are (in)appropriate behaviors directed toward other people. We'll revisit the scope problem later. For now, let's bring the evolutionary psychology of morality to bear on the cognitive science of religion.

4.2.2 Cognitive Science of Morality and the Gods

Two influential ideas that came out of the cognitive science of religion that are immediately pertinent to understanding the relationship between morality and the gods. One is that religious ideas' content contains elements that either directly violate default, modular inferences associated with certain classes of information (e.g., as they can walk through walls, a ghost is just a person that violates intuitive physics) or apply default inferences of some categories to objects in other categories (e.g., a rattle that knows where lost objects are applies mental abilities to an artifact) (Boyer & Ramble, 2001). Such ideas are the objects of our fascination, and because our attention fixates on their unusualness, these ideas are easier to remember. Because of their mnemonic advantage, these ideas are more likely to proliferate through a population (Atran, 2004; Boyer, 2007). Yet, there are many ideas that have such counterintuitive content, but aren't the targets of religious devotion. Why doesn't anyone pray to cartoon characters who regularly defy physics, cheat death, and have access to knowledge beyond their natural counterparts?

This question leads us to the second influential idea: unlike spirits and gods, other counterintuitive agents aren't endowed with "socially strategic information," a domain of useful information about other people (Boyer, 2000). It's good to know if others are honest or deceitful. It's helpful to know if someone will always be there when you need help or instead typically prioritize themselves. It's also useful to know if someone spends a little too much time in the bunker they built in their back yard. As a domain associated with cooperation, we might think of "morality" as a subset of all possible socially strategic information. According to this view, this is why we don't pray to cartoon characters: because we don't infer that their moral interest is directed toward *us*.

In theory, gods are perceived minds, and minds are by default treated as moral agents. Because we talk about gods being concerned about what we do, it comes naturally that we infer they care about how we treat each other too. If that's the case, then a few hypotheses follow. First, beliefs of morally interested, counterintuitive agents should be more memorable than mundane agents with or without access to socially strategic interest. Second, if gods are perceived *as* minds and minds are by default treated as moral agents, it follows that we should intuit that they are concerned with moral behavior. Third, people should exhibit a bias toward treating gods as moral agents even when their traditions don't explicitly and reflectively hold that gods and spirits care about morality. We still might intuit that gods know and care about human moral behavior by virtue of mind perception's relationship to moral cognition and our conduct. Fourth, if people perceive knowledgeable gods and spirits as especially attuned to moral information by virtue of default inferences, it should be easier to process an association between gods and god-like beings and socially strategic information. Using various methods, a few studies show how important this intuitive association actually is.

One study examined the relationship between prayer and sociality at the neurological level (Schjoedt et al., 2009). Using fMRI, the researchers assessed which parts of the brain were most engaged across Christian participants' recitation of The Lord's Prayer, a nursery rhyme, making personalized prayers to God, and listing wishes to Santa Claus. They found that the anterior medial prefrontal cortex – a region associated with social cognition – was the most engaged when praying to God. In other words, the brain treats interacting with deities as a social experience. If the brain treats prayer as a social act, would it also generate the inferences that the deities we pray to are moral agents?

Other research examined just how intuitive associating agents with knowledge and concern of moral information is for people. One set of experiments (Purzycki et al., 2012) measured participants' response times about what various beings knew. These beings included God, Santa Claus, an omniscient police state, and a non-interfering hyper-knowledgeable alien species. Each participant only answered questions about one of these agents (i.e., it was a between-subjects design). Questions ranged from moral questions both positive (e.g., "Does _____ know that Ann gives to the homeless?") and negative (e.g., "Does _____ know that Jane has stolen a car?") and a variety of nonmoral questions (e.g., "Does _____ know how fast Joey's heart beats?"). Participants answered questions on a computer as quickly as they could and the computer recorded how fast they answered the questions. Across these agents – all of which were treated as knowing everything – participants were quicker to answer the moral questions, with the negative questions typically the quickest. So, even though these entities were omniscient, participants' response-speeds were biased toward their knowledge of moral, socially strategic information. This suggests an important inconsistency between culturally "correct" views and how the religious mind works in real-time. But it also suggests an especially strong connection between moral domains and what gods and god-like entities know.

Recall the debates about whether the gods of traditional populations were associated with morality. All of the aforementioned cognitive studies relied on Western samples most commonly associated with Christianity. How would such studies look in other populations? Would we find similar results among individuals whose explicit beliefs pointed to things other than morality? These questions led to a group of projects conducted in the Tyva Republic, a small southern Siberian province of Russia, just north of Mongolia. Traditional Tyvan religion is associated with local spirit-masters (*cher eeleri*). These spirits are totemic, locally bound spirits that have their own territories and/or lord over particular resources (Purzycki, 2013b). A few studies (Purzycki, 2011, 2013a) show that when asked to freely list the kinds of things that anger and please *cher eeleri*, Tyvans predominantly list sullying and overexploiting nature as the primary source of spirits' anger and ritual practices as the primary source of their pleasure. Tyvans clearly associate these spirits with specific human behaviors.

Yet, when directly asked how much spirits know and care about moral information, Tyvans were consistently more likely to positively affirm that spirits knew and cared about moral behavior than they were to nonmoral information. Interestingly, these spirits' knowledge and concern were mediated by where a moral behavior took place; spirits were less knowledgeable and concerned about behaviors that transpired far away from their territories than those that occur within them. Yet, Tyvans treated them as *very* knowledgeable and concerned with moral behaviors that transpired on their territory. Notably, on average, Tyvans reported that spirits know and care more about human moral behaviors in distant places than nonmoral information that was knowable anywhere. This suggests that even though Tyvans *explicitly* and *reflectively* associate spirits with ritual and resource use, they still *intuitively* associate the same spirits with morality, particularly moral conduct in their vicinity. Put differently, when asked directly, Tyvans will explicitly think of spirits as very much "specifically supportive of human morality."

As it turns out, Tyvans do not readily list the preservation of nature or ritual participation as things that mark "good" or "bad" people (Purzycki, 2016). This suggests that the gods' concerns are not so closely related to Tyvans' *explicit* and *salient* models of morality. Yet, it is difficult to imagine that Tyvans would deny that preserving resources or paying your respects to spirits are "good" things if directly asked. In sum, this work suggests that spiritual agents and morality are at the very least *intuitively* associated, even if their most widely understood and culturally explicit concerns are about other things. If we frame one of Swanson's hypotheses in the form of a question about individual psychology and behavior, we might ask: *why would anyone come to associate gods with moral concern when they normally don't?* In other words, if it's not standard cultural fare, how do people come to express this connection?

4.2.3 Gods' Moral Associations Made Manifest

We can delineate a few candidate processes behind the observed association between gods and morality. One possibility follows from the idea that gods are treated as moral minds. If another anthropomorphic mind is interested in *some* aspect of our lives (e.g., ritual or exploiting resources), we might infer that they are concerned with how we treat others without much effort. This possibility is not so far-fetched; people might not ever think of Santa Claus as having earwax, but we can infer that he does based on the idea that he has ears and is more or less human-like. This *moral minds hypothesis* suggests that when confronted with such questions, we reason about the gods just as we do about most other interested parties (see discussion earlier) so it appears effortless to explicitly associate gods with moral concern, even if we might not normally talk about them that way (i.e., they aren't culturally widespread). We're often quick to associate misfortune with some moral failing of our own (or the immoral intentions of others), often with appeals to gods (Boyer, 2022; K. Gray & Wegner, 2010). Common sense also suggests that when we interact with new people, we don't need to be explicitly told that they don't want us to hurt or steal from them. Rather, we draw from generalizations we've cultivated throughout our lives.

Another hypothesis is the *supernatural monitoring hypothesis*. This line of work addresses how the perception of being watched alters *behavior* that could be construed as "moral." While the evidence is mixed and such experiments do not consistently tap into the obvious fact that we adjust our behavior if we feel like we're being watched (see Northover et al., 2017), a batch of research has examined how artificial indices of agency (e.g., two eyes on a computer screen, a human-like statue) alter honest or generous behaviors (Krátký et al., 2016; Nettle et al., 2013). One study (Piazza, Bering, & Ingram, 2011) of particular relevance to religion used children as participants. The children played a game where they were supposed to hit a target by throwing a ball. In this virtually impossible task, they had to play while facing away from the target. They also played alone. Half of the children were assigned this control condition. Those assigned to the treatment condition did the same task, but were initially told that a spirit inhabited the lab. The children who were told about the spirit were less likely to cheat in the task than those in the control condition. This suggests that we might intuitively associate being watched with moral interest; even though this spirit was not described as caring, these children were nevertheless more cautious about breaking the rules after entertaining that possibility (see too Bering, McLeod, & Shackelford, 2005). In such cases, spirits' moral relevance is made explicit behaviorally.

Recall Evans-Pritchard's characterization of the reflexive, "condescending" position that any moral content of small-scale societies' gods must have come from an outside influence. To the extent that the specific qualities of beliefs are transferable across gods, we might appeal to the *cultural inference hypothesis*.

Here, individuals might attribute moral concern to some gods based on what they know about other gods (indigenous or otherwise). Could it be that Tyvans associate moral concern with spirits because they also believe that the Buddha cares about (and sanctions) human morality (Purzycki & Holland, 2019)? Tyvans are certainly aware of other belief systems too (e.g., Christianity and Islam), so it is possible that they are making inferences based on their knowledge of other more explicitly moralistic traditions. This view implies that the human mind might allow such conceptual bleeding by using specific rules and deeper categories; it's as though it reasons: "if it's a spirit, then attribute moral concern to it because this other spirit cares about morality." It's plausible, but the process is unclear. Furthermore, this particular possibility does not account for why some traits are transferred across gods while others aren't. Why would one god's explicit moral interest be applied to another god when their attributed stories, appearances, and other traits are kept distinct?

Another hypothesis might be called the *projection hypothesis*, or the idea that because *we* are interested in morality, we project this interest to the gods (see Jackson & Gray, 2023). Some might hold that because we can usually query real human minds but since we can't query gods', we are likely to draw more upon our own attitudes and desires when reasoning about what gods want. One study (Epley et al., 2009) shows that with issues such as abortion, same-sex marriage, affirmative action policies, and the death penalty, Americans are more likely to align God's views with their own (over Bill Gates', George Bush's, and the average American's). It's obvious that such political attitudes are closely aligned with religious values in the American context. Would we find similar patterns in other contexts? Would Tyvan spirit-masters be more likely to care about the death penalty when individuals care about it? How far does this projection extend? Are we more likely to infer that God also has the same tastes in music and art? If so, how does this affect behavior?

Recall Swanson's hypothesis about the development of the *explicit* association between morality and the gods. He predicted that under an acute threat of moral instability, the relationship between morality and the gods will become explicit. This particular hypothesis – call it the *cooperative threat hypothesis* – suggests that the content of gods' concerns emerge in response to socially uncertain contexts as a means to influence others' behavior (see Fitouchi & Singh 2022, Fitouchi, Singh, André,& Baumard, in press). That is, to influence others, one must explicitly convey appeals. To assess the possibility that religious appeals can shift according to specific threats, one study (Purzycki, Stagnaro, & Sasaki, 2020) had Christian participants play a "Trust Game." In this experiment, participants are given some money and make a decision about whether to give it to someone else. That money is then multiplied by some factor. The recipient then makes the decision about whether to split or keep the greater sum. It's called a "Trust Game" because the initial giver has to invest some trust in the recipient in order to get a bigger payoff. In this particular experiment, Christian givers were more likely to claim that God is angered by "greed" after not getting a return. This is consistent with the *cooperative threat hypothesis*; the content of a god's concerns might be partially a response to such conditions, at least temporarily. How long such an effect would last is unknown. Further, "greed" likely falls within the general category of "morality." Would we see the same effect in contexts where people generally associate their spirits with other things like ritual and resources?

These hypotheses are neither exhaustive of the possibilities nor necessarily mutually exclusive or in competition with each other. Like the *cooperative threat hypothesis*, some of these possibilities might be more relevant in some contexts than others. As they tend to focus on specific, pan-human cognitive processes, theory in the cognitive science of religion has largely ignored variation across contexts (see Bendixen & Purzycki, 2020, 2021). Later, we'll revisit this question of context more directly (see Section 6.4.2).

To summarize, if we restrict our investigation to the level of human cognition, the relationship between morality and the gods might be characterized as follows. By treating morality as a normative system that regulates the costs and benefits of social life, we can situate the study of religious morality across biology, culture, and individual agency. Rooted in human psychology, morality and moral systems are a part of our biological heritage; as a social species, we enter the world with a considerable amount of information, particularly about expectations of how to treat others, and enculturation and reason also play a role in providing moral frameworks and scripts for moral actions. As such, that thing we call "morality" is a convoluted mix of intuitive biology, culture, and deliberate, reflective reasoning. Part of our biological heritage is also the propensity to perceive minds, and importantly, there appears to be a steadfast connection between perceiving minds and the engagement of psychological systems associated with moral reasoning. As gods are effectively treated *as* minds, we in turn treat them by default as minds with moral interests and knowledge. In other words, due to the way our minds work, the relationship between morality and the gods should be widespread, a prediction that grounds generations of anthropological observation and sentiment in human cognition.

What of religious practices? The work reviewed in this section focuses on religious and moral *beliefs*. Yet, there is a wide range of activities that people perform that are devoted to the gods. How might they relate to morality? Far from treating practices as "cognitive cheesecake," the evolutionary study of religious behavior developed the view we saw expressed earlier by Durkheim and Malinowski, namely, that to the extent that it helps to hold societies together, religious behavior is inextricably linked to morality.

5 The Evolution of Religious Behavior

Generations of evolutionary anthropologists have endorsed the view that our capacity for culture has allowed human beings to dwell in every habitable place on the planet (Binford, 1962; Richerson & Boyd, 2008).[13] Cultural traditions from house-building and hunting technologies to clothing and medicine, our ability to transmit knowledge across generations has allowed us to adapt to just about any environment. A corollary of this view is that part of the variation we see in cultural traditions stems from the kinds of problems they solve. In addition to making life possible in the natural world, some cultural traits can also address, create, and exacerbate problems in our social worlds.

What's especially interesting about humans is that we have relied on each other for a considerable amount of our evolutionary history. We're not only social, but our interdependence has contributed to our survival in critical ways. If our ability to survive and reproduce is contingent on others, it's especially important that we work together. As such, aspects of human culture likely play a critical role in overcoming threats to our social lives. Updating the cultural functionalism of Durkheim and Malinowski, evolutionary functionalists hold that some aspects of culture ensured human success through a confluence of natural and cultural selection (see Shariff, Purzycki, & Sosis, 2014). That is, some cultural traits and their variants were preserved because they contributed to human reproduction and survival in particular conditions. To some extent, then, these benefits would thus reinforce their continued transmission throughout the generations. Is religion one such adaptive technology?

In contrast to treating religion as just long, trans-generational strings of culturally learned information or an attractive by-product of our evolved psychology, a burgeoning evolutionary science suggests that religion has been and may continue to be predominantly adaptive; in a variety of ways, religious beliefs and practices contribute to human survival and reproduction (Alcorta & Sosis, 2005; Bulbulia et al., 2008; Purzycki & Sosis, 2022; Shaver et al., 2020; Slone & Van Slyke, 2016; Sosis, 2009; Wilson, 2019). As the next couple of sections review, the majority of adaptive arguments suggest that religious behaviors and beliefs contribute to the kind of cooperation that has been crucial for human success around the world. In order to further bridge the relationship between morality, cooperation, and religion, we'll first dig into

---

[13] This section draws from Purzycki and Bendixen (2025), Lightner and Purzycki (2023), and Purzycki, Bendixen, Lightner, and Sosis (2022).

the problem of cooperation and why humans are thought to be so unique in the biological world. We'll then examine the various ways in which researchers have investigated religious behavior and how that has contributed to resolving the kinds of problems that hinder moral relationships. As we'll see, these moral relationships are shaped by the way we make a living.

5.1 Evolutionary Theory and Social Life

While there are myriad forms of cross-species mutualism (Kropotkin, 1998 [1902]), one of the remarkable things about humans is that we are uniquely social and, compared to nonhuman animals, strikingly generous with each other. When it comes to investing in other individuals, most organisms tend to prioritize those most closely related to them (Hamilton, 1964). Yet, most animals don't invest much in others beyond kin; there's very little reciprocity exhibited by nonhuman animals. Human animals, however, tend to develop reciprocal relationships where nonrelated individuals will help each other out when needed and reciprocate in kind (Trivers, 1971). But human sociality also goes far *beyond* such reciprocal relationships; we regularly give considerable resources to anonymous others without ever expecting anything in return. Coupled with the fact that humanity's sociality has contributed to our survival in unprecedented ways and contexts, humans are uniquely cooperative animals. How is this possible? What role do the gods play in this process?

To get a better appreciation for the answers, let's first examine the problem of cooperation a little closer by using game theory. Evolutionary game theory (Maynard-Smith, 1982) models the evolution of competing strategies. Some game theoretic models address particular social scenarios defined by the decisions individuals make and their outcomes. These outcomes are in the form of payoffs: the costs and benefits of social decisions. In such models, individuals' payoffs are contingent on what other "players" do and how common they are in the population. The bigger your payoff, the more evolutionarily successful you are. Much of the evolutionary social sciences asks why anyone would cooperate when being selfish yields a bigger immediate payoff. You can see this in the following illustration.

Table 4 details the various payoffs of a "Prisoner's Dilemma" game. Let's say we've both done something bad and are taken to jail and thrown in separate cells. The police are pressuring us to confess to our crimes. In this game, you (Player 1) and I (Player 2) are playing against each other and payoffs in this matrix are all *your* payoffs. In this context, think of them as prison sentences. Here, b refers to "benefits" (i.e., a lighter sentence) and c means cost (i.e., a harsher sentence). Here, we assume that $b > b - c > 0 > -c$. There are two

Table 4 Payoffs for Player 1 in Prisoner's Dilemma

Player 1	Player 2 C	D
C	$b - c$	$-c$
D	b	0

strategies from which to choose. You could cooperate (C) with me by staying quiet or you could defect (D) by ratting me out. Now, if you choose C, you can get one of two payoffs, $b - c$ or $-c$, depending on what I choose. If I also cooperate, our sentence is $b - c$, but if I defect, your sentence is the harsher $-c$. If you choose D, you can either walk away with b – the lightest sentence of all or nothing at all (if I also defect). No matter the outcome, it's *always* better to choose D, or defect, because if you defect and I cooperate, you get the benefit b, but if we both defect, we get nothing.

On a grander scale, it's better for the collective if everyone cooperates. Let's say $b = 2$ and $c = 1$. That means 100 cooperators interacting only with other cooperators will get a total payoff of 100, but an all-defector sample will get nothing. On an individual level, however, it's always better to defect; 100 defectors ratting out 100 cooperators have a total payoff of 200. Because of their bigger individual payoffs, defectors will always win over cooperators. As such, there's always a looming temptation to defect. In evolutionary terms, this means defectors will eventually replace cooperators in a population.

Clearly this is not the world we live in. So, while the model nicely summarizes the problem of cooperation, it's a terrible representation of reality. Why, then, do we engage in so much cooperation? Formal mathematical theory suggests that cooperators will proliferate when they are more likely to interact with each other and when the costs of defection are high (i.e., increase the value of c).

So, we need a *mechanism* or set of mechanisms to account for how we can increase the chances that cooperators interact with each other and/or increase the costs of defecting. Research points to a wide range of mechanisms that bring (and keep) cooperators together. As already mentioned, kinship can play an important role, but the ability to keep track of cooperators and defectors is also a very important mechanism that promotes cooperation. How do we know who is likely to cooperate and who is likely to defect? If religion contributes to cooperation, it must consist of mechanisms that bring cooperators together (and keep defectors out) and/or increase the costs – real or perceived – of selfishness. The kinds of things that gods want are things that appear to do just this.

5.2 What Gods Want

What do gods want cross-culturally? We saw that there has been steadfast interest in whether they're "specifically supportive of human morality," but what about gods' other concerns? Curiously, this question managed to escape dedicated scrutiny for generations. Some early surveys are suggestive of the kinds of variation that might exist out there, but few rigorous studies exist at the level of individual beliefs. For example, Boehm (2008) surveyed forty-three ethnographies about eighteen different hunter-gatherer societies and coded the kinds of things reported to be punished by the gods. Here, Boehm made the distinction between fifteen moral behaviors (e.g., incest, murder, theft, deceit) – "antisocial" acts that are "predatory on fellow band members" (146, 148) – and eight "nonmoral taboos" (e.g., food, ritual, and sex). As it turns out, all eighteen societies had literature mentioning some form of moral behaviors condemned by the gods, though no single act beyond "deviance in general" was reported in more than half of the cases. Frequent "nonmoral taboos" discussed in the ethnographies were food, ritual, animal, and sexual taboos (cf. J. S. Brown, 1952).

Surveying various ethnographic reports, Purzycki and McNamara (2016) created a broader typology of gods' concerns. At the most general level, gods are thought to care about (*i*) things done toward other people, (*ii*) things done toward them, and (*iii*) things done toward nature. More specifically, gods care about (*i*) morality, etiquette, and virtue; (*ii*) belief and ritual; and (*iii*) resource preservation and regulation. What do these concerns have in common? What accounts for their differences?

Recent theory (Bendixen & Purzycki, 2020; Purzycki, Bendixen, et al., 2022) suggests that the cross-cultural association between gods and the behaviors they care about points to a recurring suite of features (see too McNamara & Purzycki, 2020). Specifically, these "god problems" are costly social dilemmas that are important to individuals and their communities but are difficult and/or more expensive to regulate using secular means (e.g., police, social ostracism, and other institutions). To assess these predictions, Bendixen et al. (2024) used the aforementioned categories (morality, virtue, ritual, etc.) to code data collected among over 500 individuals in eight different societies. This study asked about two gods that were important in each society. One god was pre-selected to be relatively more punitive, knowledgeable, and concerned with morality (e.g., the Abrahamic god). One was locally salient, but relatively less moralistic, punitive, and knowledgeable ("moralistic" and "local" gods, respectively). Participants listed the kinds of things that angered the gods and things that pleased them. Unsurprisingly, the "moralistic" gods were considerably more concerned with items coded as "morality" and "virtue" than the "local" gods. However, "local gods" were also consistently associated with moral issues in addition to locally specific behaviors. Moreover, as revealed by the ethnographic literature about these groups, each of the behaviors that people claimed their local gods cared about were associated with pressing social dilemmas that were difficult to regulate exclusively with secular means. This work suggests that much of the variation we see in religious traditions around the world stems from the kinds of social dilemmas people face in their communities. Furthermore, it suggests that religious behaviors are intrinsically "moral." If we go with contemporary views of morality as a regulatory system of cooperation, if gods are widely concerned with behaviors that regulate cooperation, then they are clearly "specifically supportive" of practices that contribute to moral conduct. Consistent with Malinowski's sentiments (see Section 2.3), the behaviors that people claim gods care about appear to come at individual costs in ways that benefit communities. That is, the things that gods care about are the cooperative strategies in game theoretic dilemmas. Let's take a look at a few examples up close. Given the amount of attention it has received, religious ritual offers the clearest example of gods' concerns contributing to cooperation and the moral order.

5.3 Costly Signaling Theory of Ritual

In his magnum opus, *Ritual and the Making of Humanity*, anthropologist Roy Rappaport (1999) explicitly links the moral order with ritual practice. Rappaport treats ritual as a mechanism that *establishes* and ultimately conveys acceptance of and obligation to the moral order of one's community. When someone participates in public ritual, that individual conveys to others that he or she accepts the greater tradition of which they are a part and the inherent morality of doing so. Ritual participation *"establishes an obligation* to abide by whatever conventions...that order represents. The force of acceptance is, thus, moral, for breach of obligation...is the one element present in all unethical acts" (1999, 395). Furthermore,

> failure to abide by the terms of an obligation is universally stigmatized as immoral. To the extent, then, that obligation is entailed by the acceptance intrinsic to the performance of a liturgical order, ritual establishes morality as it establishes convention. The establishment of a convention and the establishment of it morality are inextricable, if they are not, in fact, one and the same. (Rappaport, 1999, 132)

Using "morality" as norms of obligation, Rappaport details how rituals convey acceptance to tradition and their inherent moral value, namely, by conveying solidarity to the moral order that forges individuals into communities.

By *not* participating, one rejects the moral order, the greater tradition, and its constituents. As such, ritual is central to maintaining the moral order.

Some ported these insights into evolutionary theory and argued that it is the *costs* of rituals that render the message of acceptance reliable (Irons, 2001). To illustrate, first consider the tendency of male birds to have more extravagant plumage than females. It takes considerable energy to create magnificent and brightly colored feathers and having such plumage could also draw the attention of predators. Yet, females choose those males with the greatest plumage by virtue of what Zahavi and Zahavi (1999) call the "handicap principle" (see D. J. Penn & Számadó, 2020, for critical review). This principle states that paying such costs is what reliably conveys a signal of quality; ideal mates "handicap" themselves by producing and showing off apparently wasteful and often risky traits in order to demonstrate just how good they are. It's as though such birds are saying "we're so fit, we can invest in flashy, unnecessary things." Think of it as biological conspicuous consumption (Veblen, [1899] 2007). A male bird simply can't fake this kind of plumage; otherwise, low-quality males could overtake the population by faking out females.

What's this have to do with human rituals and the moral order? As Rappaport suggested, performing rituals conveys commitment to the gods *and* the moral order of one's community. Paying the *costs* of ritual is what reliably conveys that commitment. It's not enough to just say "I'm committed" or "I believe." Tattooing one's favorite slogan on one's forehead is an *obvious* demonstration of commitment to an idea. Dancing with poisonous snakes at church under the auspices of scaring away demons unquestionably conveys religious conviction. Such acts also convey solidarity with others who are a part of your group. Given all this, imagine trying to join a community that requires sacrificing a goat that you could otherwise use to feed your family. Imagine refusing to participate, apathetically standing by on the periphery of the group, or not singing or praying along with everyone else. This would likely convey a rejection of the tradition, the individuals there, and the moral order endorsed by those individuals. You aren't likely to get invited again.

Such ritual costs, then, also play a gate-keeping role; high ritual costs keep out the less-committed (Iannaccone, 1992, 1994). As such, they function as assorting dedicated cooperators, thus resolving the aforementioned problem of cooperation. Someone might try to join a cooperative group and just reap the benefits (i.e., free-ride), but is less likely to if the costs are sufficiently high. Ritual should therefore foster cooperative communities, keep out those who might otherwise exploit the benefits provided by the group, and maintain cooperation within the group by reliably conveying one's devotion. This theory generates a range of hypotheses.

First, if ritual costs reliably convey commitment, communities with more taxing rituals should outlive those with fewer and/or less costly rituals. To test this hypothesis, anthropologist Richard Sosis and psychologist Eric Bressler (2000) examined the life-span of 200 different religious and secular communes. The average age of a secular commune in the sample was 6.4 years. The average age of religious communes was 25.3, four times the lifespan of their secular counterparts. Sosis and Bressler (2003) followed up on this study with a subsample of 83 communities and found a similar pattern. Where religious communities had an average age of 35.6 years, secular communities lasted only an average of 7.7. Moreover, religious communities systematically had far more costly requirements than secular groups, including food taboos, celibacy, bans on gambling, fasts, and so forth.

Second, those who pay higher ritual costs should be more cooperative than those who don't. Many studies support this particular prediction. For instance, Sosis and Ruffle (2003) found that on average, Israeli religious kibbutz members who participated in group rituals took less money from a common pool than their secular counterparts. In Mauritius, participation in the intensely painful *kavadi* ritual induces more generous giving to charity than participation in a relatively more mundane set of rites (Xygalatas et al., 2013) and other evidence suggests that such rituals also enhance cooperation among observers, even more than participants (Mitkidis et al., 2017). One set of lab experiments (M. Lang et al., 2022) examined the social dynamics of signaling by manipulating the costs of signals by random assignment. Participants got to choose a group to play a "Public Goods Game" with. A Public Goods Game requires that individuals put in a certain amount of money into a common pool. That amount is multiplied by some factor (in this case doubled), and then redistributed equally among the participants involved. In this experiment, one group required an entry fee for everyone to convey "their intentions regarding the size of the contribution to the common pool" (8). Some of these entry fees were high and some were low. Another group required no such fee. Using a preliminary study to class individuals into selfish and cooperative types, they found that selfish participants were less likely to opt for the group that required costly entry fees. Furthermore, while they wound up not earning more than others, the individuals who opted for the group with higher entry fees wound up giving more than others.

Third, because ritual costs reliably and honestly convey one's intention to commit to the group, those who observe others paying ritual costs will perceive those individuals as more trustworthy. There are a few lines of cross-cultural evidence across a variety of methods that support this particular prediction.

In one experiment, Purzycki and Arakchaa (2013) found that when individuals in the Tyva Republic observe others who engage in communal rituals, they are more likely to rate them as honest and trustworthy, more likely to ask them to babysit, and more likely to trust that they would return borrowed and lost money. Ruffle and Sosis (2020) found that secular and religious Israelis perceive religious individuals as more trustworthy. Religiosity predicted trustworthiness *and* willingness to trust others in economic experiments in Germany (Tan & Vogel, 2008) and Brazil (Soler, 2012). In India, individuals perceive the religiously devout as being more hardworking, generous, good at giving advice, influential, and having a good character, among other positive traits (Power, 2017a). A companion study corroborates these ratings, finding that more religiously devout individuals were indeed more generous in their social networks (Power, 2017b).

Fourth, ritual costs should be especially high in contexts where the looming temptation to defect is also high. Utilizing the cross-cultural Human Relations Area Files data base (see Section 2), one study coded various ritual costs across sixty societies (Sosis, Kress, & Boster, 2007). They also treated warfare frequency as an index of the intensity of the temptation to defect; dying for others is a difficult decision to make. As predicted, the study found that societies reported as having more taxing rituals are also reported as more exposed to warfare, especially violent conflicts with other groups. Extreme rituals that leave permanent indications (e.g., circum- and subincision, tattoos, scarring, and piercing) are more prevalent in societies with external warfare.

This body of work suggests that ritual conveys one's intentions to cooperate with other group members. To the extent that the moral domain overlaps with or *is* cooperation, it suggests that the costs of ritual reliably establish one's acceptance of the moral climate of his or her group. When social ties are tested, ritual costs increase in ways that assort cooperators. Ritual is central for this function. As we'll see, culturally particular religious institutions and other practices also provide venues for bringing people together in ways that resolve locally specific threats to cooperation.

5.4 Practices, Cooperation, and Context

Ritual costs appear to contribute to human cooperation in significant ways. But what of all of the variation we see in *where* and *when* religious rituals take place (for other dimensions of variation in ritual, see Purzycki, in press; Whitehouse, 2004)? And what about the other practices that gods care about? If cultural traditions like religious ritual can contribute to the kinds of cooperation that have promoted human survival and reproduction, aspects of ritual should co-vary

Table 5 Payoffs for Player 1 in coordination in Martu field burning

Player 1	Player 2	
	Burn	Don't Burn
Burn	b	0
Don't Burn	s	s

with threats to well-being. To see the logic of this argument, let's compare two notably different traditions, the field burning practices of the Martu of Western Australia and the water temples of Balinese rice farmers.

With appeals to their ancestors and the sacred law known as "The Dreaming" (*Jukurrpa*), the Martu collectively burn expanses of fields in the western deserts (Bird et al., 2016; Bliege Bird et al., 2013). When they burn these fields together, they can keep wildfires at bay. Unlike fires started by lightning or by individuals, fires from collective burning are easier to contain. But it's arduous work and takes a lot of time and focus.

Importantly, this practice has the downstream effects of enriching the soil, thus producing seeds upon which rodents feed. Monitor lizards predate rodents and the Martu hunt the monitor lizards, ultimately distributing them to other community members (Bliege Bird & Power, 2015). As such, this tradition generates important benefits for individuals, but only when they burn together. As illustrated in Table 5, when the net benefits of burning together, b, outweigh the benefits of not bothering to chip in, s, we have a social dilemma (specifically, a "Stag Hunt"; see Bulbulia 2012 and Skyrms 2004 for further discussion). Many Martu "believe that if they do not continue to re-enact the *Jukurrpa* through emulating the creative forces of the ancestral beings across the landscape – hunting, collecting, burning and caring for family – those plants and animals that depend on their actions will cease to exist" (Bird et al., 2013, 2). In the Martu worldview, then, burning is but one component of a much larger system of moral obligation toward others. This larger system is framed in the context of living in accordance with "ancestral beings" and "The Dreaming."

Compare this to the Balinese water temple system (Lansing, 1991, 2006; Lansing & Kremer, 1993). In some areas of Bali, rice farmers plant and harvest rice on expansive terraced hill- and mountainsides where water flows from the tops of these terraces. Throughout the ages, farmers have developed a system of water and plant management that more equitably distributes water and minerals to rice paddies. How do they do this and what is the role of religious behavior? To appreciate this, let's first examine the problem.

Morality and the Gods

Table 6 Payoffs (upstream, downstream) for coordination game between farmers

	Downstream	
Upstream	Simultaneous	Staggered
Simultaneous	$1, 1-d$	$1-r, 1-r$
Staggered	$1-r, 1-r$	$1, 1-d$

As illustrated in Table 6, farmers here face a dilemma similar to the Prisoner's Dilemma. Let's say you're an upstream farmer who lives at the top of a hill. I live downstream and farm paddies closer to the bottom of the hill. If we plant our fields at the same time, you'll get all the nutrients in the water because you live closer to the source of the stream, thus leaving me with some depleted water by the time it reaches my paddies. Let's say if this happens, the water I get is depleted by d. If we think about a rice yield as some quantity, say, 1, that means you get 1 unit of rice and I get whatever remains, $1 - d$. It's in our interest to get the best water we can, so in this case, it's better for me if we stagger our planting schedule. Since the water source is continuous, why not just alternate when we plant? That way, you can use good water first and subsequently let good water you don't need flow down to me.

The problem is that our fields are also threatened by pests. If we stagger our planting schedule, your crop is likely to get infested with pests first, and then they'll just travel down to my crop after devouring yours. So, if we both stagger our planting schedule, our crops will suffer by an amount of r, but if we plant simultaneously, the pests will have nowhere to go and thus leave for better fields. So, if we choose to plant simultaneously, you are always better off, but I lose out. But if we choose to stagger our planting schedule, we both lose out due to pests. When would I, as a downstream farmer, want to coordinate with you to plant at the same time? Under these conditions, only when pests are more devastating than impoverished water (i.e., when $r > d$) will I opt for your leftovers.

Once again, the dilemma is one of coordination: *how can I get you to release some of your good water so we can coordinate planting to reduce pest infestation?* Here is where the Balinese system functions to help people coordinate. In Bali, distributed networks of "water temples" function as social institutions that foster coordination and – if the aforementioned literature is any indication – trust between farmers who are otherwise competing and coordinating around resources and their threats. During the rituals conducted at these temples, farmers pay their respects to local deities and symbolically exchange "holy water." However, it goes much more beyond symbols; each temple contributes to coordinating the harvesting and planting schedules of participating farms into superordinate collectives called *subaks*. In this way, farmers facing the challenge of coordination and/or the temptation to use the best resources right away engage in spiritually sanctioned cooperation. As it turns out, these collectives have greater rice yields than their unorganized counterparts.

Considered together, these two examples (for more, see Bendixen et al., 2024; Purzycki, Bendixen, et al., 2022) reveal some important themes. First, they illustrate how religious traditions can revolve around cooperative dilemmas that people face; it is clear that these traditions include practices that strengthen social relationships. In order to procure benefits, individuals must work together to generate them, but because doing so can come at a personal cost, there is an inherent temptation to not cooperate. Defection harms others. As such, a second theme these cases point to is the inherent moral nature of religious practices more broadly than gods' moral concerns and the moral landscape encoded in ritual. They aren't merely things that ought to be done. They also forge moral obligations, sentiments, and consist of cooperative strategies. Once again, to the extent that "morality" is a social system that facilitates cooperation, these practices – and the spiritual realm to which they appeal – are unambiguously "moral." Third, the specific dilemmas these groups face emerge as a result of the way they make a living. If cultural traditions can facilitate human survival in various conditions, it appears that these religious traditions have evolved to address various *social conditions*. This strongly suggests that elements of religion can flexibly attend to new conditions in ways that overcome cooperative challenges (Purzycki & Sosis, 2009).

Finally, while the "cooperative" strategies in these examples are behaviors believed to be endorsed by some form of spiritual entity, religious appeals contain some serious consequences for not living up to prescribed behaviors. These examples show us that problems and practices are not necessarily merely culturally *associated* with gods. Just because a god knows and care about actions that contribute to sustaining cooperation doesn't mean that an individual will actually do it or do it to the degree that's expected. Rather, the gods and their associated repercussions provide some *motivation* behind these individually costly acts. Indeed, one important motivator for religious behavior is the threat of supernatural sanctions; learning to fear spiritual consequences for violations of religious norms can propel individuals to act in ways that are individually costly, but mutually beneficial. This brings us to the Supernatural Punishment Hypothesis.

6 The Evolution of Religious Beliefs

6.1 Supernatural Punishment Hypothesis

As discussed in Section 4, one of the central ideas in the cognitive science of religion is that our unprecedented perspective-taking abilities undergird beliefs in gods. One theory suggests that because it conferred an advantage to their survival and reproduction, more and more of our distant ancestors gradually acquired this ability. Yet, the better individuals could anticipate others' thoughts and actions, the more they could influence and manipulate other people for their own benefit. So, the more one could think through others' thoughts, the more he or she could exploit them. This threatens cooperation. As we saw, without other mechanisms, Machiavellian exploiters could wind up undermining cooperation, effectively breaking down social order and proliferate.

One theory wagers that through a series of pivotal shifts in human evolution, natural selection favored individuals who were especially sensitive to threats of spiritual punishment (D. D. P. Johnson, 2016; D. D. P. Johnson & Bering, 2006; Rossano, 2007; Schloss & Murray, 2011). Drawn from this, the "supernatural punishment hypothesis" predicts that fear of gods' punishment is an important mechanism that deters defectors.

In contexts where the cost of *really* getting punished outweighs any benefit one could achieve by engaging in uncooperative behavior, defecting on cooperation is less likely. But when the potential benefits outweigh the costs, exploiting others is advantageous. Punishment can be a reliable deterrent for self-interested behavior, but punishment also comes at a cost to the punisher in the form of, for example, energy and organization (Boyd & Richerson, 1992). If that's the case, why bother risking yourself to punish other people? According to Johnson's theory, fear of supernatural punishment evolved because it motivates avoiding the *real* costs of getting punished for being selfish. Furthermore, supernatural sanctions increase the perceived costs of defecting. In other words, it pays to fear gods and it pays to promote that fear.

More formally, beliefs in supernatural punishment will come to dominate a population (i.e., evolve and proliferate) when $pc > b$, that is, when the probability of getting caught for doing something bad, p, and the costs of getting punished, c, outweigh the benefits, b, that one could get for being uncooperative. In this view, it's adaptive to fear supernatural punishment in contexts with *real* social costs for being selfish. Recall the *supernatural monitoring hypothesis* (Section 4.2.3). In addition to the costs of punishment, c, belief in supernatural punishment can also ratchet up the perception of p; even though other humans might not see what you're doing, a god most certainly can (Bourrat et al., 2011).

To test these ideas, Johnson (2005) used the SCCS using the problematic "high gods" variable (see Section 3) and various indices of cooperation. Johnson is uniquely candid about his caution regarding the difficulty of actually testing his hypothesis using the SCCS. For instance, he admits that "The ideal variable for this study would be a measure of *the extent of belief in supernatural punishment for selfishness* within each society. Unfortunately, no such variable exists in the SCCS database" (418, emphasis in original). He nevertheless proceeds to exploit the high gods variable (see Section 3) recognizing, among other things, that "not all supernatural punishment is attributed to high gods" (420) and notes how ubiquitous other forms of supernatural punishment are (432), citing Swanson (1964) as evidence. Johnson uses a host of variables to measure cooperation. Among other things, these include society size (because more cooperation means wider sustained social networks), compliance with social norms, more food sharing, and less internal strife. He found that most of the nineteen variables associated with cooperation were correlated with the high gods variable. Notably, "loyalty to the local or wider community" and "sharing of food" were *not* clearly associated with the high gods variable.

Concurrently, individual-level experimental studies addressing the relationship between belief and cooperation also picked up steam. Evidence from behavioral economics suggests that religion can promote cooperation between anonymous strangers, but it might be contingent on context. For example, Orbell et al. (1992) used a range of experimental versions of the Prisoner's Dilemma (Section 5.1) and found that Mormons were more cooperative with anonymous strangers than non-Mormons. Importantly, the Mormon sample played in a context where anonymous individuals were simply more likely to be Mormon than non-Mormon. A decade later, Shariff and Norenzayan (2007) conducted Dictator Game experiments among Canadian university students using "implicit primes." In these experiments, participants are given some money (in this case ten Canadian dollar coins) and asked to distribute them between themselves and an anonymous receiver. Half of the participants had to first solve a word scramble task that included statements such as "she felt the spirit" and "the dessert was divine" and the other half unscrambled sentences with no references to the sacred (dessert or otherwise). Those in the control condition gave an average of 1.84 coins ($SD = 1.8$), whereas those in the implicit prime condition gave just over four ($M = 4.22, SD = 2.65$). In a follow-up study, they found that a secular word-scramble task (with words like "civic," "jury," and "police") elicited a similar allocation as a religious prime condition ($M = 4.60, SD = 3.03$ coins). In another study (Shariff & Norenzayan, 2011), they found that students' beliefs in God's punishment reduced cheating whereas beliefs in a forgiving god *induced* cheating on a math test. Elsewhere, the authors cite this evidence as a demonstration of how belief in a punitive god can reduce "moral transgressions" (Norenzayan et al., 2016, 11).

Implicit and explicit priming studies have since proliferated in the study of religion and cooperation. Psychologist Azim Shariff (2015) concludes: "Does religion increase moral behavior? Yes. Even though the effect is parochial, bounded, transient, situationally constrained, and often overstated, it is real" (112). Yet, multiple attempts to replicate these studies have failed (e.g., Billingsley, Gomes, & McCullough, 2018; Gomes & McCullough, 2015) and on numerous grounds, there is increasing skepticism about their veracity (Galen, 2012). Eventually, a meta-analysis (Shariff, Willard, Andersen, & Norenzayan, 2016) examining 92 different experimental studies found a robust relationship between religious or religious-like priming and prosocial behaviors in such experimental games. While positive evidence supports the case for religious cognition containing a motivating force behind cooperation, there is a considerable amount of variation in these experiments in terms of quality, design, and focus. Indeed, there is also increased skepticism directed toward such experiments' utility *and* their subsequent inclusion in meta-analyses (see Van Elk et al., 2015). The conditions under which implicit or explicit priming can induce cooperation remains unclear and inconsistent across studies. Even if they were clear, just how far this effect extends (i.e., how broadly people apply religiously induced cooperation) also remains to be further clarified.

6.2 Moralistic Gods and Social Complexity Redux

Consider the evolutionarily recent development in human cooperation, namely, that the vast majority of us now live in large-scale state societies, regularly interacting with a multitude of anonymous, unfamiliar, and unrelated agents. In these contexts, individuals often behave in costly ways that benefit others even when there is no obvious possibility of reciprocation or even a high likelihood of punishment for noncooperative behavior (Bowles & Gintis, 2003). With so many nonreciprocal and indirect costs, how could large-scale societies maintain their cohesion? Evolutionary explanations again draw on morality as one way to resolve this particular scope problem, whether focusing on, among other things, the ability of moral behavior to signal individual qualities (see Barclay, 2013; Baumard, André, & Sperber, 2013) or actively constrain selfishness for group benefits (see Fehr, Fischbacher, & Gächter, 2002; Turchin et al., 2013).

This particular topic became increasingly trendy in the evolutionary social sciences.

Capitalizing on this trend, previous generations' efforts, and the supernatural punishment hypothesis, Norenzayan (2013) posited that so-called "big gods" were associated with "big societies" and the two co-evolved in important ways. More specifically, the more people believe gods are punitive, all-knowing, and morally concerned, the more likely they will engage in cooperative behaviors directed toward people who can't directly reciprocate. This prosociality helps societies expand since more people are willing to cooperate beyond their immediate contacts. This heightened prosociality also allows groups to organize together to dominate other groups and ultimately bring them into the fold through conquest. Increased conflict brings more people together, and such beliefs solidify such newfound alliances. Thus, in a cycle of escalation, the larger populations became, the more widespread such beliefs became, and the "bigger" the gods grew. According to the theory, this partially accounts for the global ubiquity of "big god" traditions like Christianity and Islam. This work distanced itself from Johnson's supernatural punishment hypothesis partly on the grounds that gods' punishment might have accounted for parochial cooperation and therefore relevant to more traditional religions, it did not account for the scope problem of more expansive prosociality. Gods that were more punitive, more knowledgeable, and more morally concerned were better suited for social complexity.

Simultaneously, another curious trend became a staple part of the narrative about social complexity, morality, and the gods. A spate of claims re-emerged, namely, that the religions of traditional or ancient societies had little to no connection to morality:

- "This isn't to say that hunter-gatherers never use religion to discourage troublesome or destructive behavior ... But more typical of hunter-gatherer societies is the observation...'Relations to the spirits have no ethical implication'" (Wright, 2010, 24)
- "the religions of small-scale societies including foragers often do not have one or two powerful gods who are markedly associated with moral behaviour (Roes and Raymond, 2003). Many gods are ambivalent or whimsical, even creator gods" (Shariff, Norenzayan, & Henrich, 2010, 124)
- "In most ancient traditions, the gods were generally construed as unencumbered with moral conscience and uninterested in human morality" (Baumard & Boyer, 2013, 272)
- "ancestral religions did not have a clear moral dimension" (Norenzayan, 2013, 127)
- it is "a fact that evidence for moralising gods is lacking in the majority of non-literate societies" (Whitehouse et al., 2019 [RETRACTED], 227)

- "Social scientists have long known that small-scale traditional societies – the kind missionaries used to dismiss as 'pagan' – envisaged a spirit world that cared little about the morality of human behaviour. Their concern was less about whether humans behaved nicely towards one another and more about whether they carried out their obligations to the spirits and displayed suitable deference to them" (Whitehouse et al., 2019)
- gods in small-scale societies are "weak, whimsical, and not particularly moral" (Henrich, 2020, 131).

So, after generations of debate and fieldwork that resulted in the leading anthropologists and sociologists of religion to reach the consensus view that morality is linked – in various ways – to many (if not most or virtually all) small-scale religions, these stark statements reflect a shift back to the bold generalizations Tylor (see Section 2). What happened?

One reason might be that these works drew from different definitions of constructs of "morality" pertaining to the content and scope problems. To the extent that clear and explicit definitions of "morality" are possible, they are rarely included in these works. When they are, they aren't much beyond everyday notions. For instance, one of these works suggests that "moral" refers to concerns about "behaviors that actually harm other people" (Wright, 2010, 23), but this is so general that it is quite difficult to see how this could square with the ethnographic record. Another (Norenzayan et al., 2016) provides examples of "moral transgressions" that include deceptive behaviors such as "cheating on taxes, accepting a bribe, adultery, and lying." Here, morality is not defined as generalized behaviors directed toward anyone and everyone, anonymous or otherwise. Instead, morality's scope and scale are qualified throughout (e.g., "Religious elements are not a necessary condition for cooperation or moral behavior *of any scale*," 3, or "Chiefdoms and early states predating the Axial Age[14] by thousands of years had anthropomorphized deities that intervened in social relations, although *their moral scope and powers to punish and reward were substantially narrower and more tribal* than those of later, Axial gods," 9, emphasis added). Morality can thus be *extended* to include "imagined moral communities comprising strangers," but morality is *not*

---

[14] The "Axial Age" refers to a period roughly between 800 and 200 BCE. Among others, historians of religion treat this pivotal period as one of major developments in human culture and society (Jaspers, 2014). See Section 6.3. While historian Robert Bellah (1970, 2011) makes some distinctions between "tribal," "archaic," and "Axial" traditions, he treats religion's connection to morality as common – and central – across these society types. In fact, drawing from Durkheim, he treats religion as "a system of beliefs and practices relative to the sacred that unite those who adhere to them in a moral community" (2011, p. 1, 47). Throughout his discussion of tribal religions (pp. 138–174), he finds these "moral communities" are promoted by religious myth, stories, and rituals that provide "conceptions" and "guides" to living moral lives (172), despite these phenomena lacking explicit rules or precepts.

assumed to be universalized normative behavior, but something with the capacity for expanded applicability to anonymous strangers. In sum, it doesn't appear to be the explicit conceptions of morality in these works that led them to the conclusion that small-scale traditions lack a "clear moral dimension" or that their traditional gods were "uninterested in human morality" (see too D. D. P. Johnson, 2015; Petersen, 2023).

Ultimately, these sources treat the lack of moral relevance of traditional religions as something to be explained. Rather than something with a deep and contentious history that has yet to be adequately resolved, it became an assumption used to lend support to particular theories about the growth of human societies. As such, bypassing the contentious history of this debate has rhetorical advantages. In fact, journalist Robert Wright (2010) uncritically cites Tylor (see Section 2) and specific ethnographic anecdotes as though they are representative of foragers' religions. In a footnote, Wright cites Swanson, but focuses on afterlife beliefs and claims that "In only one of those ten [hunter-gatherer societies in Swanson's data set] did the religion include any other supernatural sanctions for this sort of behavior" (490, n. 42). Yet as we saw, Swanson's data and conclusions emphatically and explicitly reject Tylor's and maintain the sentiments of the consensus reached by anthropologists of religion: moralistic supernatural punishment is fairly common among bands, tribes, and other non-state societies.

Similarly, another likely source of this shift comes from the uncritical appeal to studies exploiting the SCCS. Indeed, some cite Roes and Raymond (2003) as showing that small-scale societies lack "powerful gods who are markedly associated with moral behavior" (Shariff et al., 2010) or that "powerful moralizing gods appear in <10% of the smallest-scale human societies but become widespread in large-scale societies" (Norenzayan et al., 2016), despite Roes and Raymond (2003) relying on the dubious high gods variable. As can be seen in Table 3, virtually *all* studies reporting a positive correlation between moralistic high gods and social complexity exploit the SCCS. Unsurprisingly, many surveys cite such evidence as supporting the view that the gods of small-scale religions somehow lack an association with ethics or morality. Yet, we saw that the high gods variable has problems (e.g., not all moralistic gods are high gods) and that some of the sources that populate this dataset were created under political and methodological conditions we wouldn't accept today. Thankfully, as we have newer databases and a return to examining beliefs and behaviors in the field, there is a decreasing need to rely on the SCCS variables and data to assess the global relationship between morality and the gods.

6.3 Cross-Cultural Databases Redux

Ongoing efforts have overcome some of the problems associated with the SCCS data. For example, the Pulotu database (Watts, Sheehan, et al., 2015) includes a wide range of quantitative data coded from ethnographic materials of societies throughout Austronesia. Importantly, by taking pains not to conflate the reported *absence* of a trait and the trait not being discussed in the literature, this data set avoids many of the aforementioned pitfalls of the SCCS data. Moreover, the coding procedures are transparent. For instance, Pulotu codes "broad supernatural punishment" only when "the concept of a supernatural agent or process that reliably monitors and punishes selfish actions, and this concept must (*i*) be widely advocated within the community, (*ii*) involve punishment of a broad range of selfish behaviours and (*iii*) apply to a wide range of community members" (2).

As it turns out, while there are hardly any morally concerned *high gods* in the data set of 137 groups (only 6 societies were reported to have them), there are many instances of moralistic supernatural punishment across all societies. In fact, among the 74 societies coded has having the lowest levels of political complexity (i.e., relatively simpler chiefdoms and those societies without major heads of power), 27 were coded as having moralistic supernatural punishment (36%). Overall, 37 different groups' literatures reported broad supernatural punishment of selfish behaviors (50%). In a major study, Watts et al. (2015) examined the historical relationship between social complexity and supernatural punishment of various kinds. They found that generalized supernatural punishment is more likely to predate social complexity than moralistic high gods. The latter appear *after* social complexity emerges, but since only three of the six societies with moralistic high gods were coded as complex, there are very little data with which to draw inferences.

Another database, Seshat, was developed to assess societal evolution through history and pre-history. Instead of focusing on cultural groups like the SCCS and Pulotu, Seshat initially included data coded from historical records of various geographic regions through time, which means that if other traditions colonize the particular area, there is little to say about the evolution of specific traditions. Using this database, one article (Whitehouse et al., 2019 [RETRACTED]) assessed the historical relationship between social complexity and moralistic supernatural punishment. The farther back in time we go, the less information we have. The historical record is virtually barren before the advent of writing and archaeological evidence rarely provides unambiguous examples of morally concerned gods (e.g., see Raffield, Price, & Collard, 2019; Rossano, 2023). As such, there was very little data with which to work.

In fact, 61% of all of the possible data points for moralizing gods simply had no data.

By way of handling these unknown values, the researchers converted all of these cases for moralistic supernatural punishment into zeros, thus treating moralistic supernatural punishment as "absent." Since the bulk of these values were for historically deep societies of relatively low social complexity, this maneuver provided the very answer the study was designed to assess. Going back through time, societies were simpler and lacked data. Before testing whether such societies have moralistic gods, the researchers declared them to be absent. Thus, nearly 500 absent data points drove the result: small-scale societies far back in time don't have moralistic gods. Among other issues (see Beheim et al., 2021; Shin et al., 2019), this particular problem contributed to the paper's subsequent retraction.

The report's public retraction notice frames the issue as a mistake in the data itself rather than the conversion that took place during analysis (Whitehouse et al., 2021). A subsequent report (Turchin et al., 2023b) uses a newer version of the data set where virtually all of the values that were originally unknown were converted to "inferred absent" (Purzycki, Bendixen, & Lightner, 2023). These "inferred absent" values were subsequently recoded and merged with "absent" values; 463 out of 471–98.3%–of data now treated as "absent" were actually "inferred absent" values which were almost entirely missing from the original data set. Now citing historians and various sources commenting on the target societies to justify the "inferred" absences, the new report finds a similar result, namely, that there is no evidence that moralistic supernatural punishment causes social complexity.

The authors note that

> the study of world history demonstrates that...the primary mode of religion of early and small-scale social formations, are less likely to be highly moralizing. In [such] systems, morality is situational and communal. While some aspects of the supernatural may be connected to pro-social norms in these societies (such as ideas about loyalty to kin), these religions tend to lack abstract, universalizing ethical codes. (Turchin et al., 2023a, 226)

Of course, no previous study equates moralistic supernatural punishment with "abstract, universalizing ethical codes." Furthermore, their admittedly "high standard" of morality being the "primary concern" in such traditions would constrain any analysis by virtue of its narrowness (see Fitouchi, André, & Baumard, 2023), not to mention the difficulty of ascertaining it in the historical and archaeological records of ancient small-scale populations. Given how much of this "demonstration" is inferred, more concrete answers await further inquiry.

In addition to ignorance, part of the suite of problems inherent in such studies lies in the fact these databases rely on coarse, group-level data that are not crafted from systematic studies conducted among individuals (see Section 3.3). Yet, we know that there can be considerable variation *within* groups, just as there is variation *between* them (D'Andrade, 1987). Furthermore, many studies seek to draw inferences about individual behavior, not population characteristics. Sometimes, relationships at the group level mask or even run counter to traits at the individual level. Take, for example, the suggestion that wealthy people are attracted to moralistic religions because the wealthy use such beliefs to justify their judgment of the poor's behavior. Using historical data, Baumard et al. (2015) found that increases in ancient societies' projected wealth in the form of per capita/diem kilocalories brought them to the so-called "Axial Age" (see note 14), a period often associated with the rise of "moralistic traditions" like Buddhism, Confucianism, Christianity, and Islam. Using individual-level data from different groups around the world, one study (Purzycki, Ross, et al., 2018) found the same thing at the level of groups; average food security of a group predicted its average rating of how morally concerned deities were. However, there was no relationship at the level of individuals; the degree to which *individuals* worried about procuring food was in no way associated with the degree to which they claimed their gods cared about theft, murder, and deceit (for further discussion, see Mullins et al., 2018). Indeed, it appears that when we conduct individual-level studies in the field, we are compelled to revisit the conclusions of previous generations of anthropologists. That is, gods' association with morality is just not that rare among the world's different religions.

6.4 Supernatural Punishment in the Field

6.4.1 Effects of Beliefs

Despite the mixed evidence from the group-level historical and ethnographic databases, individual-level data collected in the field strongly suggests that supernatural punishment can contribute to cooperation and its expansion. For example, economists Hadnes and Schumacher (2012) conducted Trust Games in villages in Burkina Faso of sub-Saharan Africa. They study found that not only did traditional religious beliefs include supernatural punishment of moral transgressions including dishonesty and theft, but also that those endorsing such beliefs contributed more on average in the Trust Game. Cultural psychologist Rita McNamara brought an experiment to Yasawa, Fiji (McNamara, Norenzayan, & Henrich, 2016). Focusing on the Christian deity and local ancestor spirits, she assessed if beliefs in these gods' punishment predicted equitable distributions of money in a game that measured honest play. She reasoned that because the Christian god is associated with generalized morality and the local spirits are associated more with community norms, when people believe they are more punitive than kind, individuals will alter their behavior accordingly.

In her experiments, participants were instructed to allocate thirty coins to two different individuals designated by cups using a fair two-colored die. First, they had to think of which cup they wanted to put a coin into. If the die came up one color, participants were supposed to put the coin into the cup of which they mentally chose. If the die came up the other color, they were supposed to put the coin into the cup opposite to what they had in mind. Participants knew that the money would go to whomever was described on the cups, including themselves. If followed, these rules would generate a random coin allocation (hence "Random Allocation Game"); it wouldn't matter which cup players thought of because there was a random chance a coin would go into any given cup. However, individuals played alone and could easily put as many coins into whichever cup they wanted. The assumption, then, is that individuals will bias their allocations to benefit themselves and local community members at the expense of distant co-religionists. And they do. If participants deviate from chance allocations, one can see systematic overall deviations with statistical analysis (Hruschka et al., 2014). Among other things, the more participants claimed God and the ancestor spirits punished, the more they played fairly toward anonymous strangers (note that these results were contingent on how much participants worried about having enough food to eat).

Expanding this work, *The Evolution of Religion and Morality Project* (M. Lang et al., 2024; Purzycki, Henrich, & Norenzayan, 2024) measured individual responses to a wide range of questions regarding beliefs and practices. After selecting two focal deities (again, the "moralistic" and "local" from Section 5.2) on the basis of quantitative ethnographic data, this team of researchers carried out behavioral economic experiments across fifteen societies. These experiments consisted of at most two experimental Random Allocation Games, and another that measured generosity, a Dictator Game where participants simply allocated an amount of money to other individuals and kept the rest. Overall, the more people claimed their gods knew and punished people, the more they played fairly and generously toward anonymous, geographically distant people who shared the same religious affiliation (for further discussion, see M. Lang et al., 2019; Purzycki et al., 2016). That is, the more individuals claimed their gods knew and punished, the more they exhibited the kind of anonymous and expansive cooperation required to sustain large-scale societies. Recent cross-cultural evidence (Pasek et al., 2023) using a Dictator Game suggests that simply having participants think about God can increase generosity even toward religious outgroups.

However, these studies did *not* find that *moralistic* gods promote cooperation any more or broader than relatively less moralistic "local" gods (Purzycki, Lang, Henrich, & Norenzayan, 2022). In fact, the degree to which people claimed their gods cared about morality did *not* predict behavior much at all. Across scale questions asking how often such gods punished theft, deceit, and murder, free-response methods asking what angers and pleases the target gods, and a wide range of analyses, how "moralistic" gods were was of *no clear consequence* to cooperation (Bendixen et al., 2023). Furthermore, the experimental design did not allow a comparison between tradition types. Recipients on the cups were typically described as co-religionists *of the tradition associated with moralistic gods* (e.g., the Christian god or Hindu Shiva) rather than local traditions (e.g., spirit-masters or ancestor spirits). It is also important to note that these studies still exhibited considerable cross-cultural variation. While individuals were more likely to offer money when they believed their gods to be knowledgeable and punitive, some sites showed far more (or less) cooperation than others. In fact, some of the most selfish behavior in these experiments were among those thoroughly steeped in Christianity (e.g., Yasawa; see Fig. 2). This suggests that factors beyond beliefs are playing an important role in accounting for religious prosociality and its absence.

In sum, we still lack evidence that "moralistic gods" specifically promote cooperation in ways any different from the other gods. Yet, supernatural punishment and monitoring beliefs of various gods *are* associated with cooperating beyond parochial boundaries. This suggests that the age-old hyper-emphasis of gods' "moral concern" – universal, parochial, "primary," anonymous, or otherwise – is an otiose factor in promoting cooperation. And, when we look at individual-level data from real, living people, it becomes even clearer that the very construct of a "moralistic god," the theories ostensibly striving to account for them, and the methods typically deployed in their assessment deserve serious reconsideration.

6.4.2 "Local" Gods Punish Immoral Behavior

Recall the findings recounted earlier, where indigenous Siberians from the Tyva Republic were – when asked – resoundingly inclined to associate their gods with knowledge and concern of human moral conduct (Purzycki, 2011, 2013a). Using data collected in the *Evolution of Religion and Morality Project*, Purzycki et al. (2022) followed up on this line of work. They found that across 13 traditions' "local" gods (i.e., those selected to be less morally

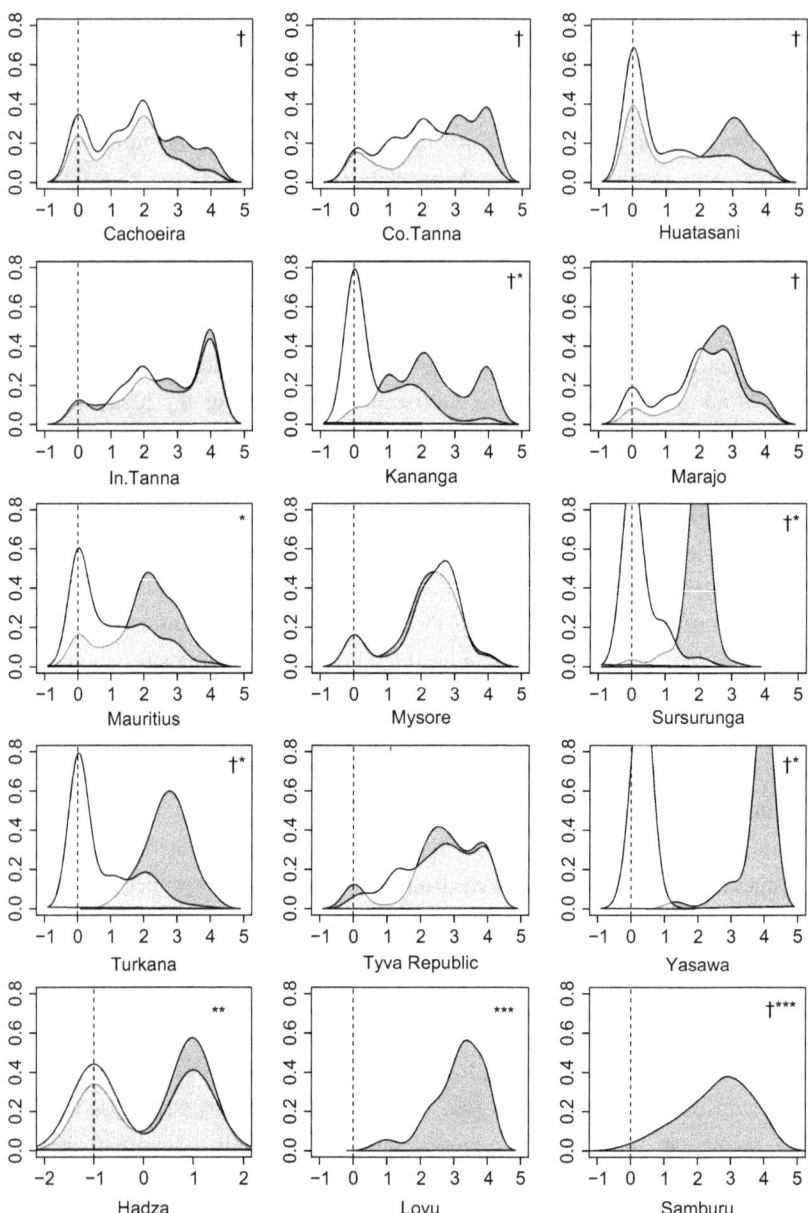

Figure 2 Density plots of mean moralistic punitive interest scores of "moralistic" (gray) and "local" (white) gods across fifteen populations

Note: Dotted line marks bottom of the scale (minimum was 0, maximum was 4).
†Moralistic god is Christian deity; *Commitment to local deity is illegal, taboo, or frowned upon; **Hadza used a different scale to answer question; ***No local deity data provided
Source: Figure adapted from Lightner et al. (2023).

concerned, knowledgeable, and punitive), participants rated nearly all of them as morally punitive to a significant degree. Yet, even the so-called "moralistic gods" weren't always rated as especially moralistic. Figure 2 shows the density plots of average responses to a three-item "moral interest scale" across fifteen sites.

What about the *cultural inference hypothesis* (see Section 4.2.3)? Did responses about "local gods" simply reflect beliefs about the "moralistic gods"? In most cases, the overlap between the "moralistic" and the "local" gods on these scales are virtually complete. That is, the correlation between the ratings of the two gods in each site were quite strong. Yet, as it turns out, the likelihood of claiming local gods punish moral infractions holds after statistically holding constant this correlation. Furthermore, the solitary group of hunter-gatherers in the sample, the Hadza foragers of Tanzania, were asked to freely list the kinds of things that anger two of their deities (*Ishoko* and *Haine*, associated with the moon and sun respectively). Items coded as "morality" were the most common items listed across both gods. There was no clear relationship between listing moral items and individuals' exposure to missionaries.

In fact, the exceptions to associating "local" gods with moralistic punishment – most clearly seen in Mauritius (where local spirits were the *nam* associated with black magic), and among the Kananga, Sursurunga, Turkana, and Yasawans (where participants answered questions about ancestor spirits) – are contexts where engaging in practices devoted to such deities is either illegal or where the dominant religion (typically Christian, as denoted by the crosses in the upper corners of each plot) sanctions against or competes with the "local" tradition. Given what we know about some of the missionary and other reports used in cross-cultural datasets, this particular finding should be unsurprising. The default god, then, appears to be moralistic. Exceptions are accounted for when dominant traditions have deemed such spirits *immoral* to engage!

A clutch of other important examples from field research further suggest that the gods of small-scale or non-world religions are unambiguously associated with morality. For example, after getting reminders of supernatural punishment of local spirits thought to "bring misfortune to individuals who fail to share with others and reward those who are especially generous" (Townsend et al., 2020, 3), Ik (Uganda) participants were more generous to needy, anonymous community members than those in a control condition. Singh et al. (2021) found that the horticultural Mentawai on Siberut Island, Indonesia, believe in a local spirit called Sikameinan who punishes people when they don't share food, particularly hunted meat. If an infraction occurs, individuals can host rituals that involve food sharing and public apologies for being greedy. It appears, then, that the insights gleaned from generations of dedicated cross-cultural fieldwork are re-confirmed with contemporary fieldwork. In addition to bolstering the insights and observations of generations past, empirical substantiations of this relationship using contemporary methods are also adding important nuance to the narratives about the relationship between morality and the gods. As the field appears to be just warming up to this possibility, there's a considerable amount of work that remains to be done.

7 Conclusion

From the edicts of the Ur-Nammu and Hammurabi to the theories and methods of the social sciences, the tangled relationship between the gods and how we treat each other has inspired some major cultural achievements. Indeed, 4,000 years after the Sumerians, the social sciences still find the relationship between morality and the gods a source of inspiration (and frustration). This Element suggests that the story – our theories and how we go about assessing them – needs, once again, to be rewritten.

To synthetically summarize the most current evidence reviewed in this text, then, we might say – variation in theoretical and operational definitions notwithstanding – that:

> humans perceive gods that play a role in human lives as minds that are interested in their behaviour. Around the world, individuals readily associate their gods with moral interest and punishment of moral infractions. While beliefs in gods' punishment and knowledge can motivate cooperation in ways that go beyond one's local community, the degree to which they are thought to punish immoral behaviour as of yet shows no clear relationship to corresponding behaviour. Religious rituals can contribute to cooperation as their costs reliably convey that one is committed to one's group and moral norms, while other religious behaviours can contribute to specific, local threats to cooperation, thus promoting within-group prosociality and curbing selfishness.

Instead of being tenuously connected to common aspects of moral life or only present in the globalized religions, important elements of religion from all walks of human life are *intrinsically* linked to moral systems (Teehan, 2020) and the use and distribution of resources (see Atran et al., 2002; Hartberg, Cox, & Villamayor-Tomas, 2016). And, it appears that gods' explicit associations with morality are more common around the world than is often thought. For all intents and purposes, the gods' relationship to morality is varied, but constant: beliefs might harness the kinds of psychological systems that promote interpersonal conduct, religious narratives describe and portray how people ought to comport themselves, and the sense of obligation and group solidarity religious behaviors convey are all part of religions' ethical dimensions. Research continues to probe the relationship at various analytical levels:

- **cognition and belief**: gods' intuitive associations with moral concern
- **beliefs and individuals**: if and how beliefs in supernatural punishment and monitoring induce individually costly behaviors that promote cooperation
- **beliefs and society**: if and how beliefs in moralistic supernatural punishment and monitoring promote cooperation beyond direct reciprocal transactions
- **practices and individuals**: how participation in costly rituals promotes trust and cooperation within communities
- **practices and society**: if religious behaviors are cooperative strategies in locally specified social dilemmas
- **society and resources**: what role religious traditions play in how societies manage and distribute resources

Of course, the study of this relationship continues to evolve; from how we conceive and operationalize to how we measure and theorize, it's clear that the conversation will continue to be re-crafted. Future work should vigilantly ask: *What do our theories actually predict? Do they speak to intuitive or reflective beliefs? Individual or group beliefs? How do/don't our methods tap into them? Are we measuring ancient beliefs or just distilled, erroneous representations of them? What do our experiments have to do with the real world?* At the end of the day, we must also ask: *so what?* If gods tend to be moralistic at least intuitively, does it have anything to do with how we treat each other or we have adapted to new environments? Considerable research suggests that the gods do matter, but research and casual observation also suggest that the gods are unnecessary devices that bolster morality. If gods are optimal solutions to cooperative threats, evidence of this possibility remains to be seen. While research in secularization (e.g., Inglehart, 2020) continues to probe the conditions under which the gods' sway on our moral lives dwindles, there is plenty to learn – and apparently time to learn it – before that happens completely.

References

Alcorta, C. S., & Sosis, R. (2005). Ritual, emotion, and sacred symbols: The evolution of religion as an adaptive complex. *Human Nature*, *16*(4), 323–359.

Alexander, R. D. (1987). *The Biology of Moral Systems*. New Brunswick: Aldine Transaction.

Atkinson, Q. D., & Bourrat, P. (2011). Beliefs about god, the afterlife and morality support the role of supernatural policing in human cooperation. *Evolution and Human Behavior*, *32*(1), 41–49.

Atran, S. (2004). *In Gods We Trust: The Evolutionary Landscape of Religion*. Oxford: Oxford University Press.

Atran, S., Medin, D., Ross, N. et al. (2002). Folkecology, cultural epidemiology, and the spirit of the commons: A garden experiment in the Maya Lowlands. *Current Anthropology*, *43*(3), 421–450.

Barclay, P. (2013). Strategies for cooperation in biological markets, especially for humans. *Evolution and Human Behavior*, *34*(3), 164–175.

Barkow, J. H., Cosmides, L., & Tooby, J. (1995). *The Adapted Mind: Evolutionary Psychology and the Generation of Culture*. Oxford: Oxford University Press.

Baron-Cohen, S. (1997). *Mindblindness: An Essay on Autism and Theory of Mind*. Cambridge, MA: MIT Press.

Barrett, J. L. (2004). *Why Would Anyone Believe in God?* Lanham: AltaMira Press.

Barrett, J. L., & Keil, F. C. (1996). Conceptualizing a nonnatural entity: Anthropomorphism in God concepts. *Cognitive Psychology*, *31*(3), 219–247.

Baumard, N., André, J.-B., & Sperber, D. (2013). A mutualistic approach to morality: The evolution of fairness by partner choice. *Behavioral and Brain Sciences*, *36*(01), 59–78.

Baumard, N., & Boyer, P. (2013). Explaining moral religions. *Trends in Cognitive Sciences*, *17*(6), 272–280.

Baumard, N., Hyafil, A., Morris, I., & Boyer, P. (2015). Increased affluence explains the emergence of ascetic wisdoms and moralizing religions. *Current Biology*, *25*(1), 10–15.

Beheim, B., Atkinson, Q. D., Bulbulia, J. et al. (2021). Treatment of missing data determined conclusions regarding moralizing gods. *Nature*, *595*(7866), E29–E34.

Bellah, R. N. (1970). Religious Evolution. In S. N. Eisenstadt (Ed.), *Readings in Social Evolution and Development* (pp. 211–244). Oxford: Pergamon.

Bellah, R. N. (2011). *Religion in Human Evolution: From the Paleolithic to the Axial Age.* Cambridge: Belknap Press.

Bendixen, T., Apicella, C., Atkinson, Q. et al. (2024). Appealing to the minds of gods: Religious beliefs and appeals correspond to features of local social ecologies. *Religion, Brain & Behavior, 14*(2), 183–205.

Bendixen, T., Lightner, A. D., Apicella, C. et al. (2023). Gods are watching and so what? Moralistic supernatural punishment across 15 cultures. *Evolutionary Human Sciences, 5*, e18.

Bendixen, T., & Purzycki, B. G. (2020). Peering into the minds of gods: What cross-cultural variation in gods' concerns can tell us about the evolution of religion. *Journal for the Cognitive Science of Religion, 5*(2), 142–165.

Bendixen, T., & Purzycki, B. G. (2021). Competing forces account for the stability and evolution of religious beliefs. *The International Journal for the Psychology of Religion, 31*(4), 307–312.

Bentzen, J. S., & Gokmen, G. (2022). The power of religion. *Journal of Economic Growth, 28*(1), 45–78.

Bering, J. M., McLeod, K., & Shackelford, T. K. (2005). Reasoning about dead agents reveals possible adaptive trends. *Human Nature, 16*(4), 360–381.

Billingsley, J., Gomes, C. M., & McCullough, M. E. (2018). Implicit and explicit influences of religious cognition on dictator game transfers. *Royal Society Open Science, 5*(8), 170238.

Binford, L. R. (1962). Archaeology as anthropology. *American Antiquity, 28*(2), 217–225.

Bird, D. W., Bliege Bird, R., Codding, B. F., & Taylor, N. (2016). A landscape architecture of fire: cultural emergence and ecological pyrodiversity in Australia's Western Desert. *Current Anthropology, 57*(S13), S65–S79.

Bliege Bird, R. B., & Power, E. A. (2015). Prosocial signaling and cooperation among Martu hunters. *Evolution and Human Behavior, 36*(5), 389–397.

Bliege Bird, R. B., Tayor, N., Codding, B. F., & Bird, D. W. (2013). Niche construction and dreaming logic: Aboriginal patch mosaic burning and varanid lizards (*Varanus gouldii*) in Australia. *Proceedings of the Royal Society B: Biological Sciences, 280*(1772), 20132297.

Boehm, C. (1980). Exposing the moral self in Montenegro: The use of natural definitions to keep ethnography descriptive. *American Ethnologist, 7*(1), 1–26.

Boehm, C. (1993). Egalitarian behavior and reverse dominance hierarchy. *Current Anthropology, 34*(3), 227–254.

Boehm, C. (2008). A biocultural evolutionary exploration of supernatural sanctioning. In J. Bulbulia, R. Sosis, E. Harris, R. Genet, & K. Wyman (Eds.), *Evolution of Religion: Studies, Theories, and Critiques* (pp. 143–152). Santa Margarita: Collins Foundation Press.

Botero, C. A., Gardner, B., Kirby, K. R. et al. (2014). The ecology of religious beliefs. *Proceedings of the National Academy of Sciences*, *111*(47), 16784–16789.

Bourrat, P., Atkinson, Q. D., & Dunbar, R. I. (2011). Supernatural punishment and individual social compliance across cultures. *Religion, Brain & Behavior*, *1*(2), 119–134.

Bouton, J. (1635). *An Account of the Establishment of the French in the Year 1635 on the Island of Martinique* (McKusick & P. Verin, Trans.). Paris: Chez S. Cramoisy. https://ehrafworldcultures.yale.edu/ehrafe/citation.do?method=citation&forward=browseAuthorsFullContext&id=st13-003.

Bowles, S., & Gintis, H. (2003). Origins of human cooperation. In P. Hammerstein (Ed.), *Genetic and Cultural Evolution of Cooperation* (pp. 429–443). Cambridge, MA: The MIT Press.

Boyd, R., & Richerson, P. J. (1992). Punishment allows the evolution of cooperation (or anything else) in sizable groups. *Ethology and Sociobiology*, *13*(3), 171–195.

Boyer, P. (2000). Functional origins of religious concepts: Ontological and strategic selection in evolved minds. *Journal of the Royal Anthropological Institute*, *6*(2), 195–214.

Boyer, P. (2007). *Religion Explained: The Evolutionary Origins of Religious Thought*. New York: Basic Books.

Boyer, P. (2022). Why we blame victims, accuse witches, invent taboos, and invoke spirits: A model of strategic responses to misfortune. *Journal of the Royal Anthropological Institute*, *28*(4), 1345–1364.

Boyer, P., & Ramble, C. (2001). Cognitive templates for religious concepts: Cross-cultural evidence for recall of counter-intuitive representations. *Cognitive Science*, *25*(4), 535–564.

Breton, R. (1929 [1635–1647]). *An Account of the Island of Guadaloupe* (T. Armand de Turner, Trans.). Paris: Librairie GTnTrale et Internationale. https://ehrafworldcultures.yale.edu/document?id=st13-001.

Brown, C., & Eff, E. A. (2010). The state and the supernatural: Support for prosocial behavior. *Structure and Dynamics*, *4*(1). https://escholarship.org/uc/item/5rh6z6z6.

Brown, J. S. (1952). A comparative study of deviations from sexual mores. *American Sociological Review*, *17*(2), 135–146.

Bulbulia, J. (2012). Spreading order: Religion, cooperative niche construction, and risky coordination problems. *Biology & Philosophy, 27*(1), 1–27.

Bulbulia, J., Sosis, R., Harris, E. et al. (2008). *The Evolution of Religion: Studies, Theories, & Critiques*. Santa Margarita: Collins Foundation Press.

Call, J., & Tomasello, M. (2008). Does the chimpanzee have a theory of mind? 30 years later. *Trends in Cognitive Sciences, 12*(5), 187–192.

Caton, C. E. (1963). In what sense and why "ought"–judgements are universalizable. *The Philosophical Quarterly, 13*(50), 48–55.

Chomsky, N. (1965). *Aspects of the Theory of Syntax*. Cambridge, MA: MIT Press.

Chudek, M., McNamara, R. A., Birch, S., Bloom, P., & Henrich, J. (2018). Do minds switch bodies? Dualist interpretations across ages and societies. *Religion, Brain & Behavior, 8*(4), 354–368.

Cosmides, L., & Tooby, J. (2005). Neurocognitive adaptations designed for social exchange. In D. M. Buss (Ed.), *The Handbook of Evolutionary Psychology* (pp. 584–627). Hoboken: John Wiley and Sons.

Cronk, L. (1994). Evolutionary theories of morality and the manipulative use of signals. *Zygon, 29*(1), 81–101.

Cronk, L. (1998). Ethnographic text formation processes. *Social Science Information, 37*(2), 321–349.

Curry, O. S. (2016). Morality as cooperation: A problem-centred approach. In T. K. Shackelford & R. D. Hansen (Eds.), *The Evolution of Morality* (pp. 27–51). Leiden: Springer.

Curry, O. S., Chesters, M. J., & Van Lissa, C. J. (2019). Mapping morality with a compass: Testing the theory of "morality-as-cooperation" with a new questionnaire. *Journal of Research in Personality, 78*, 106–124.

Curry, O. S., Mullins, D. A., & Whitehouse, H. (2019). Is it good to cooperate? Testing the theory of morality-as-cooperation in 60 societies. *Current Anthropology, 60*(1), 47–69.

D'Andrade, R. G. (1987). Modal responses and cultural expertise. *American Behavioral Scientist, 31*(2), 194–202.

Danielson, A. J., Arbuckle MacLeod, C., Hamm, M. J. et al. (2022). Testing and disrupting ontologies: Using the Database of Religious History as a Pedagogical Tool. *Religions, 13*(9), 1–29.

Darwin, C. (1871). *The Descent of Man*. Princeton: Penguin Classics.

Dobrizhoffer, M. (1822). *An Account of the Abipones, an Equestrian People of Paraguay* (Vol. 2). London: John Murray. https://ehrafworldcultures.yale.edu/document?id=si04-001.

Dow, M. M., & Eff, E. A. (2009). Multiple imputation of missing data in cross-cultural samples. *Cross-Cultural Research, 43*(3), 206–229.

Dunn, O., & Kelley Jr., J. E. (1989). *The Diario of Christopher Columbus's First Voyage to America, 1492–1493*. Norman: University of Oklahoma Press.

Durkheim, E. (2001 [1912]). *The Elementary Forms of Religious Life*. Oxford: Oxford University Press.

Eastman, C. A. (1911). *The Soul of the Indian: An Interpretation*. Lincoln: University of Nebraska Press.

Ember, C. R. (2007). Using the HRAF collection of ethnography in conjunction with the Standard Cross-Cultural Sample and the Ethnographic Atlas. *Cross-Cultural Research, 41*(4), 396–427.

Ember, C. R., Skoggard, I., Felzer, B., Pitek, E., & Jiang, M. (2021). Climate variability, drought, and the belief that high gods are associated with weather in nonindustrial societies. *Weather, Climate, and Society, 13*(2), 259–272.

Epley, N., Converse, B. A., Delbosc, A., Monteleone, G. A., & Cacioppo, J. T. (2009). Believers' estimates of God's beliefs are more egocentric than estimates of other people's beliefs. *Proceedings of the National Academy of Sciences, 106*(51), 21533–21538.

Evans-Pritchard, E. E. (1956). *Nuer Religion*. Oxford: Oxford University Press.

Evans-Pritchard, E. E. (1965). *Theories of Primitive Religion*. Oxford: Clarendon Press.

Fehr, E., Fischbacher, U., & Gächter, S. (2002). Strong reciprocity, human cooperation, and the enforcement of social norms. *Human Nature, 13*(1), 1–25.

Fessler, D. M. T., Barrett, H. C., Kanovsky, M. et al. (2015, August). Moral parochialism and contextual contingency across seven societies. *Proceedings of the Royal Society B, 282*(1813), 20150907.

Fitouchi, L., André, J.- B., & Baumard, N. (2023). From supernatural punishment to big gods to puritanical religions: Clarifying explanatory targets in the rise of moralizing religions. *Religion, Brain & Behavior, 13*(2), 195–199.

Fitouchi, L., & Singh, M. (2022). Supernatural punishment beliefs as cognitively compelling tools of social control. *Current Opinion in Psychology, 44*, 252–257.

Fitouchi, L., Singh, M., André, J.- B., & Baumard, N. (in press). Prosocial religions as folk-technologies of mutual policing. *Psychological Review*.

Fodor, J. A. (1983). *The Modularity of Mind*. Cambridge, MA: MIT Press.

Galen, L. W. (2012). Does religious belief promote prosociality? A critical examination. *Psychological Bulletin, 138*(5), 876–906.

Gardner, P. M. (1972). The paliyans. In M. G. Bicchieri (Ed.), *Hunters and Gatherers Today: A Socioeconomic Study of Eleven Such Cultures in the Twentieth Century* (pp. 404–447). Prospect Heights: Wavelend Press.

Ge, E., Chen, Y., Wu, J., & Mace, R. (2019). Large-scale cooperation driven by reputation, not fear of divine punishment. *Royal Society Open Science, 6*(8), 190991.

Gomes, C. M., & McCullough, M. E. (2015). The effects of implicit religious primes on dictator game allocations: A preregistered replication experiment. *Journal of Experimental Psychology: General, 144*(6), e94.

Graham, J., Haidt, J., Koleva, S. et al. (2013). Moral foundations theory: The pragmatic validity of moral pluralism. *Advances in Experimental Social Psychology, 47*, 55–130.

Gray, J. P. (1987). Do women have higher social status in hunting societies without high gods? *Social Forces, 65*(4), 1121–1131.

Gray, K., & Pratt, S. (2025). Morality in our mind and across cultures and politics. *Annual Review of Psychology, 76*, 663–691.

Gray, K., & Wegner, D. (2010). Blaming God for our pain: Human suffering and the divine mind. *Personality and Social Psychology Review, 14*(1), 7–16.

Gray, K., Young, L., & Waytz, A. (2012). Mind perception is the essence of morality. *Psychological Inquiry, 23*(2), 101–124.

Greene, J. (2013). *Moral Tribes: Emotion, Reason, and the Gap between Us and Them.* New York: Penguin.

Guthrie, S. E. (1980). A cognitive theory of religion. *Current Anthropology, 21*(2), 181–203.

Guthrie, S. E. (1995). *Faces in the Clouds: A New Theory of Religion.* New York: Oxford University Press.

Guthrie, S. E. (2000). On animism. *Current Anthropology, 41*(1), 106–107.

Hadnes, M., & Schumacher, H. (2012). The gods are watching: An experimental study of religion and traditional belief in Burkina Faso. *Journal for the Scientific Study of Religion, 51*(4), 689–704.

Haidt, J., & Kesebir, S. (2010). Morality. In S. Fiske & D. Gilbert (Eds.), *Handbook of Social Psychology* (5th ed., pp. 797–832). Hoboken: Wiley.

Hamilton, W. (1964). The genetical evolution of social behaviour I. *Journal of Theoretical Biology, 7*(1), 1–16.

Hanke, L. (1951). *Bartolomé de las Casas: An Interpretation of His Life and Writings.* Dordrecht: Springer.

Harper, R. F. (1904). *The Code of Hammurabi* (2nd ed.). Chicago: University of Chicago Press.

Harris, M. (1968). *The Rise of Anthropological Theory: A History of Theories of Culture*. New York: Thomas Y. Crowell.

Hartberg, Y., Cox, M., & Villamayor-Tomas, S. (2016). Supernatural monitoring and sanctioning in community-based resource management. *Religion, Brain & Behavior*, 6(2), 95–111.

Helm, J. (1972). The Dogrib Indians. In M. G. Bicchieri (Ed.), *Hunters and Gatherers Today: A Socioeconomic Study of Eleven Such Cultures in the Twentieth Century* (pp. 51–89). Prospect Heights: Wavelend Press.

Henrich, J. (2020). *The WEIRDest People in the World: How the West Became Psychologically Peculiar and Particularly Prosperous*. New York: Penguin.

Hirschfeld, L. A., & Gelman, S. A. (1994). *Mapping the Mind: Domain Specificity in Cognition and Culture*. Cambridge: Cambridge University Press.

Hruschka, D., Efferson, C., Jiang, T. et al. (2014). Impartial institutions, pathogen stress and the expanding social network. *Human Nature*, 25, 567–579.

Iannaccone, L. R. (1992). Sacrifice and stigma: Reducing free-riding in cults, communes, and other collectives. *Journal of Political Economy*, 100(2), 271–291.

Iannaccone, L. R. (1994). Why strict churches are strong. *American Journal of Sociology*, 99(5), 1180–1211.

Imuta, K., Henry, J. D., Slaughter, V., Selcuk, B., & Ruffman, T. (2016). Theory of mind and prosocial behavior in childhood: A meta-analytic review. *Developmental Psychology*, 52(8), 1192.

Inglehart, R. F. (2020). *Religion's Sudden Decline: What's Causing It, and What Comes Next?* Oxford: Oxford University Press.

Irons, W. (2001). Religion as a hard-to-fake sign of commitment. In R. M. Nesse (Ed.), *Evolution and the Capacity for Commitment* (pp. 292–309).

Izquierdo, C., Johnson, A., & Shepard Jr, G. H. (2008). Revenge, envy and sorcery in an Amazonian society. In S. Beckerman & P. Valentine (Eds.), *Revenge in the Cultures of Lowland South America* (pp. 162–186). Gainsville: University of Florida Press.

Jackson, J. C., Gelfand, M., & Ember, C. R. (2020). A global analysis of cultural tightness in non-industrial societies. *Proceedings of the Royal Society B*, 287(1930), 20201036.

Jackson, J. C., & Gray, K. (2023). The divine projector: How human motivations and biases give shape to gods' minds. In B. G. Purzycki & T. Bendixen (Eds.), *The Minds of Gods: New Horizons in the Naturalistic Study of Religion* (pp. 29–40). London: Bloomsbury Press.

Jaspers, K. (2014). *The Origin and Goal of History*. London: Routledge.
Johnson, A. (2003). *Families of the Forest: The Matsigenka Indians of the Peruvian Amazon*. Berkeley: University of California Press.
Johnson, D. D. P. (2005). God's punishment and public goods. *Human Nature*, *16*(4), 410–446.
Johnson, D. D. P. (2015). Big gods, small wonder: Supernatural punishment strikes back. *Religion, Brain & Behavior*, *5*(4), 290–298.
Johnson, D. D. P. (2016). *God is Watching You: How the Fear of God Makes Us Human*. Oxford: Oxford University Press.
Johnson, D. D. P., & Bering, J. (2006). Hand of god, mind of man: Punishment and cognition in the evolution of cooperation. *Evolutionary Psychology*, *4*(1), 147470490600400119.
Kahneman, D. (2003). A perspective on judgment and choice: Mapping bounded rationality. *The American Psychologist*, *58*(9), 697–720.
Kant, I. (1997 [1785]). *Groundwork of the Metaphysics of Morals* (M. J. Gregor, Ed.). Cambridge: Cambridge University Press.
Kaplan, H. S., Hooper, P. L., & Gurven, M. (2009). The evolutionary and ecological roots of human social organization. *Philosophical Transactions of the Royal Society B: Biological Sciences*, *364*(1533), 3289–3299.
Krátký, J., McGraw, J. J., Xygalatas, D., Mitkidis, P., & Reddish, P. (2016). It depends who is watching you: 3-D agent cues increase fairness. *PloS One*, *11*(2), e0148845.
Kropotkin, P. (1998 [1902]). *Mutual Aid: A Factor of Evolution*. London: Freedom Press.
Lang, A. (1909). *The Making of Religion*. London: Longmans.
Lang, M., Chvaja, R., Purzycki, B. G., Václavík, D., & Staněk, R. (2022). Advertising cooperative phenotype through costly signals facilitates collective action. *Royal Society Open Science*, *9*(5), 202202.
Lang, M., Purzycki, B. G., Apicella, C. L. et al. (2019). Moralizing gods, impartiality and religious parochialism across 15 societies. *Proceedings of the Royal Society B*, *286*(1898), 20190202.
Lang, M., Purzycki, B. G., Henrich, J., & Norenzayan, A. (2024). *The Evolution of Religion and Morality* (Vol. 2). London: Routledge.
Lansing, J. S. (1991). *Priests and Programmers: Technologies of Power in the Engineered Landscape of Bali*. Princeton: Princeton University Press.
Lansing, J. S. (2006). *Perfect Order: Recognizing Complexity in Bali*. Princeton: Princeton University Press.
Lansing, J. S., & Kremer, J. N. (1993). Emergent properties of Balinese water temple networks: Coadaptation on a rugged fitness landscape. *American Anthropologist*, *95*(1), 97–114.

Lawson, E. T., & McCauley, R. N. (1993). *Rethinking Religion: Connecting Cognition and Culture*. Cambridge: Cambridge University Press.

Lee, R. B. (2003). *The Dobe Ju/'hoansi*. Belmont: Wadsworth

Liénard, P., & Boyer, P. (2006). Whence collective rituals? A cultural selection model of ritualized behavior. *American Anthropologist, 108*(4), 814–827.

Lightner, A. D., Bendixen, T., & Purzycki, B. G. (2023). Moralistic supernatural punishment is probably not associated with social complexity. *Evolution and Human Behavior, 44*(6), 555–565.

Lightner, A. D., & Purzycki, B. G. (2023). Game theoretical aspects of the minds of gods. In B. G. Purzycki & T. Bendixen (Eds.), *The Minds of Gods: New Horizons in the Naturalistic Study of Religion* (pp. 133–147). London: Bloomsbury

Machery, E., & Mallon, R. (2010). Evolution of morality. In J. M. Doris (Ed.), *The Moral Psychology Handbook* (pp. 3–46). Oxford: Oxford University Press.

Malinowski, B. (1944). *A Scientific Theory of Culture and Other Essays*. Chapel Hill: University of North Carolina Press.

Malinowski, B. (2014). *Malinowski and the Work of Myth* (I. Strenski, Ed.). Princeton: Princeton University Press.

Malle, B. F., & Robbins, P. (2025). *The Cambridge Handbook of Moral Psychology*. Cambridge: Cambridge University Press.

Maynard-Smith, J. (1982). *Evolution and the Theory of Games*. Cambridge: Cambridge University Press.

McNamara, R. A., Norenzayan, A., & Henrich, J. (2016). Supernatural punishment, in-group biases, and material insecurity: Experiments and ethnography from Yasawa, Fiji. *Religion, Brain & Behavior, 6*(1), 34–55.

McNamara, R. A., & Purzycki, B. G. (2020). Minds of gods and human cognitive constraints: socio-ecological context shapes belief. *Religion, Brain & Behavior, 10*(3), 223–238.

Mitkidis, P., Ayal, S., Shalvi, S. et al. (2017). The effects of extreme rituals on moral behavior: The performers-observers gap hypothesis. *Journal of Economic Psychology, 59*, 1–7.

Morgan, L. H. (1877). *Ancient Society or Researches in the Lines of Human Progress from Savagery, through Barbarism to Civilization*. New York: Henry Holt.

Mullins, D. A., Hoyer, D., Collins, C. et al. (2018). A systematic assessment of "Axial Age" proposals using global comparative historical evidence. *American Sociological Review, 83*(3), 596–626.

Murdock, G. P. (1957). World ethnographic sample. *American Anthropologist, 59*(4), 664–687.

Murdock, G. P. (1967). Ethnographic Atlas: A summary. *Ethnology*, *6*(2), 109–236.

Murdock, G. P., & White, D. R. (1969). Standard Cross-Cultural Sample. *Ethnology*, *8*(4), 329–369.

Naroll, R. (1961). Two solutions to Galton's problem. *Philosophy of Science*, *28*(1), 15–39.

Naroll, R. (1965). Galton's problem: The logic of cross-cultural analysis. *Social Research*, *63*, 428–451.

Naroll, R., & Naroll, F. (1963). On bias of exotic data. *Man*, *63*(1), 24–26.

Nettle, D., Harper, Z., Kidson, A. et al. (2013). The watching eyes effect in the dictator game: It's not how much you give, it's being seen to give something. *Evolution and Human Behavior*, *34*(1), 35–40.

Norenzayan, A. (2013). *Big gods: How Religion Transformed Cooperation and Conflict*. Princeton: Princeton University Press.

Norenzayan, A., Shariff, A. F., Gervais, W. M. et al. (2016). The cultural evolution of prosocial religions. *Behavioral and Brain Sciences*, *39*, e1.

Northover, S. B., Pedersen, W. C., Cohen, A. B., & Andrews, P. W. (2017). Artificial surveillance cues do not increase generosity: Two meta-analyses. *Evolution and Human Behavior*, *38*(1), 144–153.

Ohnuki-Tierney, E. (1981). *Illness and Healing among the Sakhalin Ainu: A Symbolic Interpretation*. Cambridge: Cambridge University Press. https://ehrafworldcultures.yale.edu/cultures/ab06/documents/013.

Orbell, J., Goldman, M., Mulford, M., & Dawes, R. (1992). Religion, context, and constraint toward strangers. *Rationality and Society*, *4*(3), 291–307.

Pasek, M. H., Kelly, J. M., Shackleford, C. et al. (2023). Thinking about god encourages prosociality toward religious outgroups: A cross-cultural investigation. *Psychological Science*, *34*(6), 657–669.

Penn, D. C., & Povinelli, D. J. (2007). On the lack of evidence that non-human animals possess anything remotely resembling a 'theory of mind'. *Philosophical Transactions of the Royal Society B: Biological Sciences*, *362*(1480), 731–744.

Penn, D. J., & Számadó, S. (2020). The handicap principle: How an erroneous hypothesis became a scientific principle. *Biological Reviews*, *95*(1), 267–290.

Peoples, H. C., Duda, P., & Marlowe, F. W. (2016). Hunter-gatherers and the origins of religion. *Human Nature*, *27*(3), 261–282.

Peoples, H. C., & Marlowe, F. W. (2012). Subsistence and the evolution of religion. *Human Nature*, *23*(3), 253–269.

Peregrine, P. (1996). The Birth of the Gods revisited: A partial replication of Guy Swanson's (1960) cross-cultural study of religion. *Cross-Cultural Research*, *30*(1), 84–112.

Petersen, A. K. (2023). From watching human acts to penetrating their souls. In B. G. Purzycki & T. Bendixen (Eds.), *The Minds of Gods: New Horizons in the Naturalistic Study of Religion* (pp. 101–110). London: Bloomsbury.

Piazza, J., Bering, J. M., & Ingram, G. (2011). "Princess Alice is watching you": Children's belief in an invisible person inhibits cheating. *Journal of Experimental Child Psychology*, *109*(3), 311–320.

Pinker, S. (1997). *How the Mind Works*. London: W. W. Norton.

Power, E. A. (2017a). Discerning devotion: Testing the signaling theory of religion. *Evolution and Human Behavior*, *38*(1), 82–91.

Power, E. A. (2017b). Social support networks and religiosity in rural South India. *Nature Human Behaviour*, *1*(3), 0057.

Purzycki, B. G. (2011). Tyvan *cher eezi* and the socioecological constraints of supernatural agents' minds. *Religion, Brain & Behavior*, *1*(1), 31–45.

Purzycki, B. G. (2013a). The minds of gods: A comparative study of supernatural agency. *Cognition*, *129*(1), 163–179.

Purzycki, B. G. (2013b). Toward a cognitive ecology of religious concepts: An example from the Tyva Republic. *Journal for the Cognitive Science of Religion*, *1*(1), 99–120.

Purzycki, B. G. (2016). The evolution of gods' minds in the Tyva Republic. *Current Anthropology*, *57*(S13), S88–S104.

Purzycki, B. G. (in press). Some of the understudied dimensions of ritual. *Journal for the Cognitive Science of Religion*.

Purzycki, B. G., Apicella, C., Atkinson, Q. D. et al. (2016). Moralistic gods, supernatural punishment and the expansion of human sociality. *Nature*, *530*(7590), 327–330.

Purzycki, B. G., & Arakchaa, T. (2013). Ritual behavior and trust in the Tyva Republic. *Current Anthropology*, *54*(3), 381–388.

Purzycki, B. G., & Bendixen, T. (2025). Moral and religious systems. In B. Malle & P. A. Robbins (Eds.), *Cambridge Handbook of Moral Psychology* (pp. 575–595). Cambridge: Cambridge University Press.

Purzycki, B. G., Bendixen, T., & Lightner, A. D. (2023). Coding, causality, and statistical craft: The emergence and evolutionary drivers of moralistic supernatural punishment remain unresolved. *Religion, Brain & Behavior*, *13*(2), 207–214.

Purzycki, B. G., Bendixen, T., Lightner, A. D., & Sosis, R. (2022). Gods, games, and the socioecological landscape. *Current Research in Ecological and Social Psychology*, *3*, 100057.

Purzycki, B. G., Finkel, D. N., Shaver, J. et al. (2012). What does God know? Supernatural agents' access to socially strategic and non-strategic information. *Cognitive Science*, *36*(5), 846–869.

Purzycki, B. G., Henrich, J., & Norenzayan, A. (2024). *The Evolution of Religion and Morality* (Vol. 1). London: Routledge.

Purzycki, B. G., & Holland, E. C. (2019). Buddha as a god: An empirical assessment. *Method & Theory in the Study of Religion*, *31*(4-5), 347–375.

Purzycki, B. G., Lang, M., Henrich, J., & Norenzayan, A. (2022). The evolution of religion and morality project: Reflections and looking ahead. *Religion, Brain & Behavior*, *12*(1–2), 190–211.

Purzycki, B. G., & McKay, R. (2023). Morality, gods, and social complexity. In B. G. Purzycki & T. Bendixen (Eds.), *The Minds of Gods: New Horizons in the Naturalistic Study of Religion* (pp. 121–132). London: Bloomsbury Press.

Purzycki, B. G., & McNamara, R. A. (2016). An ecological theory of gods' minds. In De Cruz, H., Nichols, R., & Beebe, J. R. (Eds.), *Advances in Religion, Cognitive Science, and Experimental Philosophy* (pp. 143–167). London: Bloomsbury.

Purzycki, B. G., Pisor, A., Apicella, C. et al. (2018). The cognitive and cultural foundations of moral behavior. *Evolution and Human Behavior*, *39*(5), 490–501.

Purzycki, B. G., Ross, C. T., Apicella, C. et al. (2018). Material security, life history, and moralistic religions: A cross-cultural examination. *PloS One*, *13*(3), e0193856.

Purzycki, B. G., & Sosis, R. (2009). The religious system as adaptive: Cognitive flexibility, public displays, and acceptance. In Voland, E., & Schiefenhövel, W. (Eds.), *The Biological Evolution of Religious Mind and Behavior* (pp. 243–256). Leiden: Springer.

Purzycki, B. G., & Sosis, R. (2022). *Religion Evolving: Cultural, Cognitive, and Ecological Dynamics*. Sheffield: Equinox.

Purzycki, B. G., Stagnaro, M. N., & Sasaki, J. (2020). Breaches of trust change the content and structure of religious appeals. *Journal for the Study of Religion, Nature and Culture*, *14*(1), 71–94.

Purzycki, B. G., & Watts, J. (2018). Reinvigorating the comparative, cooperative ethnographic sciences of religion. *Free Inquiry*, *38*(3), 26–29.

Purzycki, B. G., & Willard, A. K. (2016). MCI theory: A critical discussion. *Religion, Brain & Behavior*, *6*(3), 207–248.

Purzycki, B. G., Willard, A. K., Klocová, E. K. et al. (2022). The moralization bias of gods' minds: a cross-cultural test. *Religion, Brain & Behavior*, *12*(1-2), 38–60.

Raffield, B., Price, N., & Collard, M. (2019). Religious belief and cooperation: A view from Viking-Age Scandinavia. *Religion, Brain & Behavior*, *9*(1), 2–22.

Rappaport, R. A. (1999). *Ritual and Religion in the Making of Humanity*. Cambridge: Cambridge University Press.

Richerson, P. J., & Boyd, R. (2008). *Not by Genes Alone: How Culture Transformed Human Evolution*. Chicago: University of Chicago Press.

Roes, F. L. (2014). Permanent group membership. *Biological Theory*, *9*(3), 318–324.

Roes, F. L., & Raymond, M. (2003). Belief in moralizing gods. *Evolution and Human Behavior*, *24*(2), 126–135.

Rossano, M. J. (2007). Supernaturalizing social life: Religion and the evolution of human cooperation. *Human Nature*, *18*, 272–294.

Rossano, M. J. (2010). *Supernatural Selection: How Religion Evolved*. Oxford: Oxford University Press.

Rossano, M. J. (2023). The minds behind the ritual: How "ordering gods" reinforced human cooperation. In B. G. Purzycki & T. Bendixen (Eds.), *The Minds of Gods: New Horizons in the Naturalistic Study of Religion* (pp. 77–88). London: Bloomsbury Press.

Ruffle, B. J., & Sosis, R. H. (2020). Do religious contexts elicit more trust and altruism? Decision-making scenario experiments. *Journal of Economics, Management and Religion*, *1*(1), 1–25.

Sanderlin, G. W. (1992). *Witness: Writings of Bartolomé de las Casas*. Maryknoll: Orbis Books.

Sanderson, S. K., & Roberts, W. W. (2008). The evolutionary forms of the religious life: A cross-cultural, quantitative analysis. *American Anthropologist*, *110*(4), 454–466.

Schebesta, P., & Schütze, F. (1957). Negritos of Asia; vol. 2, Ethnography of the Negritos: Half-Vol. 1, Religion and Mythology. In *Studia instituti anthropos* (Vol. 13, pp. HRAF ms: vi, 405 [original: xiv, 336]). Wien-Mödling: St. -Gabriel-Verlag. https://ehrafworldcultures.yale.edu/document?id=an07-002 (Paul Schebesta).

Schjoedt, U., Stødkilde-Jørgensen, H., Geertz, A. W., & Roepstorff, A. (2009). Highly religious participants recruit areas of social cognition in personal prayer. *Social Cognitive and Affective Neuroscience*, *4*(2), 199–207.

Schlebusch, C. M., Malmström, H., Günther, T. et al. (2017). Southern African ancient genomes estimate modern human divergence to 350,000 to 260,000 years ago. *Science*, *358*(6363), 652–655.

Schloss, J. P., & Murray, M. J. (2011). Evolutionary accounts of belief in supernatural punishment: A critical review. *Religion, Brain & Behavior*, *1*(1), 46–99.

Schwartz, S. H. (2007). Universalism values and the inclusiveness of our moral universe. *Journal of Cross-Cultural Psychology*, *38*(6), 711–728.

Schwimmer, E. G. (1973). *Exchange in the Social Structure of the Orokaiva: Traditional and Emergent Ideologies in the Northern District of Papua*. London: C. Hurst & Co. https://ehrafworldcultures.yale.edu/document?id=oj23-005.

Service, E. R. (1962). *Primitive Social Organization: An Evolutionary Perspective* (2nd ed.). New York: Random House.

Shariff, A. F. (2015). Does religion increase moral behavior? *Current Opinion in Psychology*, *6*, 108–113.

Shariff, A. F., & Norenzayan, A. (2007). God is watching you: Priming god concepts increases prosocial behavior in an anonymous economic game. *Psychological Science*, *18*(9), 803–809.

Shariff, A. F., & Norenzayan, A. (2011). Mean gods make good people: Different views of god predict cheating behavior. *The International Journal for the Psychology of Religion*, *21*(2), 85–96.

Shariff, A. F., Norenzayan, A., & Henrich, J. (2010). The birth of high gods: How the cultural evolution of supernatural policing agents influenced the emergence of complex, cooperative human societies, paving the way for civilization. In M. Schaller, A. Norenzayan, S. J. Heine, T. Yamagishi, & T. Kameda (Eds.), *Evolution, Culture and the Human Mind* (pp. 119–136). New York: Psychology Press.

Shariff, A. F., Purzycki, B. G., & Sosis, R. (2014). Religions as cultural solutions to social living. In A. B. Cohen (Ed.), *Culture Reexamined: Broadening Our Understanding of Social and Evolutionary Influences* (pp. 217–238). Washington, DC: APA Books.

Shariff, A. F., Willard, A. K., Andersen, T., & Norenzayan, A. (2016). Religious priming: A meta-analysis with a focus on prosociality. *Personality and Social Psychology Review*, *20*(1), 27–48.

Shaver, J. H., Power, E. A., Purzycki, B. G. et al. (2020). Church attendance and alloparenting: An analysis of fertility, social support and child development among English mothers. *Philosophical Transactions of the Royal Society B*, *375*(1805), 20190428.

Shin, J., Price, M. H., Wolpert, D. et al. (2019). Human societies first grow, then improve their information processing, then grow some more. *Preprint: SocArXiv*. https://osf.io/ejfbm.

Shweder, R. A., Much, N. C., Mahapatra, M., & Park, L. (1997). The "big three" of morality (autonomy, community, divinity) and the "big three" explanations of suffering. In A. M. Brandt & P. Rozin (Eds.), *Morality and Health* (pp. 119–169). London: Taylor & Frances/Routledge.

Silberbauer, G. B. (1972). The G/wi Bushmen. In M. G. Bicchieri (Ed.), *Hunters and Gatherers Today: A Socioeconomic Study of Eleven Such Cultures in the Twentieth Century* (pp. 271–326). Prospect Heights: Wavelend Press.

Simpson, J. H. (1984). High gods and the means of subsistence. *Sociological Analysis, 45*(3), 213–222.

Singh, M., Kaptchuk, T. J., & Henrich, J. (2021). Small gods, rituals, and cooperation: The Mentawai water spirit Sikameinan. *Evolution and Human Behavior, 42*(1), 61–72.

Skoggard, I., Ember, C. R., Pitek, E., Jackson, J. C., & Carolus, C. (2020). Resource stress predicts changes in religious belief and increases in sharing behavior. *Human Nature, 31*(3), 249–271.

Skyrms, B. (2004). *The Stag Hunt and the Evolution of Social Structure*. Cambridge: Cambridge University Press.

Slone, D. J. (2007). *Theological Incorrectness: Why Religious People Believe What They Shouldn't*. Oxford: Oxford University Press.

Slone, D. J., & Van Slyke, J. A. (2016). *The Attraction of Religion: A New Evolutionary Psychology of Religion*. London: Bloomsbury.

Snarey, J. (1996). The natural environment's impact upon religious ethics: A cross-cultural study. *Journal for the Scientific Study of Religion, 35*(2), 85–96.

Soler, M. (2012). Costly signaling, ritual and cooperation: Evidence from Candomblé, an Afro-Brazilian religion. *Evolution and Human Behavior, 33*(4), 346–356.

Sørensen, J. F., & Purzycki, B. G. (2023). Animatism reconsidered: A cognitive perspective. In B. G. Purzycki & T. Bendixen (Eds.), *The Minds of Gods: New Horizons in the Naturalistic Study of Religion* (pp. 63–75). London: Bloomsbury Press.

Sosis, R. (2000). Religion and intragroup cooperation: Preliminary results of a comparative analysis of utopian communities. *Cross-Cultural Research, 34*(1), 70–87.

Sosis, R. (2009). The adaptationist-byproduct debate on the evolution of religion: Five misunderstandings of the adaptationist program. *Journal of Cognition and Culture, 9*(3–4), 315–332.

Sosis, R., & Bressler, E. R. (2003). Cooperation and commune longevity: A test of the costly signaling theory of religion. *Cross-Cultural Research*, *37*(2), 211–239.

Sosis, R., Kress, H. C., & Boster, J. S. (2007). Scars for war: Evaluating alternative signaling explanations for cross-cultural variance in ritual costs. *Evolution and Human Behavior*, *28*(4), 234–247.

Sosis, R., & Ruffle, B. J. (2003). Religious ritual and cooperation: Testing for a relationship on Israeli religious and secular kibbutzim. *Current Anthropology*, *44*(5), 713–722.

Sperber, D. (1996). *Explaining Culture: A Naturalistic Approach*. Oxford: Blackwell.

Sperber, D. (1997). Intuitive and reflective beliefs. *Mind & Language*, *12*(1), 67–83.

Stark, R. (2001). Gods, rituals, and the moral order. *Journal for the Scientific Study of Religion*, *40*(4), 619–636.

Swanson, G. E. (1964). *The Birth of the Gods: The Origin of Primitive Beliefs*. Ann Arbor: University of Michigan Press.

Tan, J. H., & Vogel, C. (2008). Religion and trust: An experimental study. *Journal of Economic Psychology*, *29*(6), 832–848.

Teehan, J. (2020). Religion and morality: The evolution of a cognitive nexus. In J. R. Liddle & T. K. Shackelford (Eds.), *The Oxford Handbook of Evolutionary Psychology and Religion* (pp. 117–134). Oxford: Oxford University Press.

Tomasello, M., & Vaish, A. (2013). Origins of human cooperation and morality. *Annual Review of Psychology*, *64*, 231–255.

Townsend, C., Aktipis, A., Balliet, D., & Cronk, L. (2020). Generosity among the Ik of Uganda. *Evolutionary Human Sciences*, *2*(e23).

Trivers, R. L. (1971). The evolution of reciprocal altruism. *The Quarterly Review of Biology*, *46*(1), 35–57.

Turchin, P., Brennan, R., Currie, T. E. et al. (2015). Seshat: The global history databank. *Cliodynamics: The Journal of Quantitative History and Cultural Evolution*, *6*(1), 77–107.

Turchin, P., Currie, T. E., Turner, E. A., & Gavrilets, S. (2013). War, space, and the evolution of old world complex societies. *Proceedings of the National Academy of Sciences*, *110*(41), 16384–16389.

Turchin, P., Whitehouse, H., Larson, J. et al. (2023a). Big gods and big science: Further reflections on theory, data, and analysis. *Religion, Brain & Behavior*, *13*(2), 218–231.

Turchin, P., Whitehouse, H., Larson, J. et al. (2023b). Explaining the rise of moralizing religions: A test of competing hypotheses using the Seshat databank. *Religion, Brain & Behavior*, *13*(2), 1–28.

Turiel, E. (1983). *The Development of Social Knowledge: Morality and Convention*. Cambridge: Cambridge University Press.

Turiel, E. (2006). Thought, emotions, and social interactional processes in moral development. In M. Killen & J. Smetana (Eds.), *Handbook of Moral Development* (pp. 7–35). Mahwah: Lawrence Erlbaum Associates.

Turner, L. M. (1894). *Ethnology of the Ungava district, Hudson Bay Territory*. Washington, DC: Government Printing Office. https://www.gutenberg.org/ebooks/39659.

Tylor, E. B. (1871a). *Primitive Culture: Researches into the Development of Mythology, Philosophy, Religion, Art and Custom* (Vol. 1). J. Murray.

Tylor, E. B. (1871b). *Primitive Culture: Researches into the Development of Mythology, Philosophy, Religion, Art and Custom* (Vol. 2). J. Murray.

Tylor, E. B. (1889). On a method of investigating the development of institutions; applied to laws of marriage and descent. *The Journal of the Anthropological Institute of Great Britain and Ireland*, *18*, 245–272.

Tylor, E. B. (1892). On the limits of savage religion. *The Journal of the Anthropological Institute of Great Britain and Ireland*, *21*, 283–301.

Underhill, R. (1975). Economic and political antecedents of monotheism: A cross-cultural study. *American Journal of Sociology*, *80*(4), 841–861.

Van Elk, M., Matzke, D., Gronau, Q. F. et al. (2015). Meta-analyses are no substitute for registered replications: A skeptical perspective on religious priming. *Frontiers in Psychology*, *6*, 1365.

Veblen, T. ([1899] 2007). *The Theory of the Leisure Class*. Oxford: Oxford University Press.

Walker, J. R. (1980). *Lakota Belief and Ritual*. Lincoln: University of Nebraska Press.

Wallace, A. (1966). *Religion: An Anthropological View*. New York: Random House.

Watts, J., Greenhill, S. J., Atkinson, Q. D. et al. (2015, April). Broad supernatural punishment but not moralizing high gods precede the evolution of political complexity in Austronesia. *Proceedings of the Royal Society of London B: Biological Sciences*, *282*(1804), 20142556.

Watts, J., Jackson, J. C., Arnison, C. et al. (2022). Building quantitative cross-cultural databases from ethnographic records: Promise, problems and principles. *Cross-Cultural Research*, *56*(1), 62–94.

Watts, J., Sheehan, O., Greenhill, S. J. et al. (2015). Pulotu: Database of Austronesian supernatural beliefs and practices. *PloS One*, *10*(9), e0136783.

White, C. (2021). *An Introduction to the Cognitive Science of Religion: Connecting Evolution, Brain, Cognition and Culture.* New York: Routledge.

White, C. J., Kelly, J. M., Shariff, A. F., & Norenzayan, A. (2019). Supernatural norm enforcement: Thinking about karma and God reduces selfishness among believers. *Journal of Experimental Social Psychology, 84,* 103797.

Whitehouse, H. (2004). *Modes of Religiosity: A Cognitive Theory of Religious Transmission.* Walnut Creek: Rowman Altamira.

Whitehouse, H., François, P., Savage, P. E. et al. (2019 [RETRACTED]). Complex societies precede moralizing gods throughout world history. *Nature, 568*(7751), 226.

Whitehouse, H., François, P., Savage, P. E. et al. (2021). Retraction note: Complex societies precede moralizing gods throughout world history. *Nature.* www.nature.com/articles/s41586-021-03656-3.

Whitehouse, H., Savage, P., Turchin, P., & Francois, P. (2019). Big gods came after the rise of civilisations, not before, finds study using huge historical database. *The Conversation, 20.* https://theconversation.com/big-gods-came-after-the-rise-of-civilisations-not-before-finds-study-using-huge-historical-database-113801.

Wilson, D. (2019). *Darwin's Cathedral: Evolution, Religion, and the Nature of Society.* Chicago: University of Chicago Press.

Wright, R. (2010). *The Evolution of God: The Origins of Our Beliefs.* New York: Little, Brown.

Xygalatas, D., Mitkidis, P., Fischer, R. et al. (2013). Extreme rituals promote prosociality. *Psychological Science, 24*(8), 1602–1605.

Young, L., & Phillips, J. (2011). The paradox of moral focus. *Cognition, 119*(2), 166–178.

Zahavi, A., & Zahavi, A. (1999). *The Handicap Principle: A Missing Piece of Darwin's Puzzle.* Oxford: Oxford University Press.

Acknowledgments

Many thanks go to Adam Baimel, Bret Beheim, Theiss Bendixen, Joe Henrich, Josh Jackson, Martin Lang, Aaron Lightner, Ryan McKay, Rita McNamara, Ara Norenzayan, Anne Pisor, Cody Ross, Joni Sasaki, Nick Stagnaro, Richard Sosis, Olivier van Baars, and Joseph Watts for their collaborations on these topics over the past few years. I thank Jonathan Jong for his encouragement and the editorial care he took with this volume. Many thanks also go to Daniel Major-Smith, Richard Sosis, Connor Wood, and to the two reviewers, whose careful reading and constructive feedback were very helpful. I gratefully acknowledge the Aarhus University Research Foundation and the Templeton Religion Trust (#TRT-2022-31107) for generous support as I worked on this manuscript. I'd like to dedicate this work to Jessica McCutcheon, an exquisite example of how one can be good without a god.

Cambridge Elements

Psychology of Religion

Jonathan Lewis-Jong
St Mary's University Twickenham and University of Oxford

Jonathan Lewis-Jong is Researcher in Psychology of Religion at the Benedict XVI Centre for Religion and Society at St Mary's University, Twickenham, and an Associate of the Ian Ramsey Centre for Science and Religion at the University of Oxford. His recent books include *Experimenting with Religion* (2023) and *Death Anxiety and Religion Belief* (2016). He is also an Associate Editor at the American Psychological Association journal *Psychology of Religion and Spirituality*.

Editorial Board
Paul Bloom, *University of Toronto*
Adam B. Cohen, *Arizona State University*
Ara Norenzayan, *University of British Columbia*
Crystal Park, *University of Connecticut*
Aiyana Willard, *Brunel University*
Jacqueline Woolley, *University of Texas at Austin*

About the Series
This series offers authoritative introductions to central topics in the psychology of religion, covering the psychological causes, consequences, and correlates of religion, as well as conceptual and methodological issues. The Elements reflect diverse perspectives, including from developmental, evolutionary, cognitive, social, personality and clinical psychology, and neuroscience.

Cambridge Elements ≡

Psychology of Religion

Elements in the Series

Divination: A Cognitive Perspective
Ze Hong

Morality and the Gods
Benjamin Grant Purzycki

A full series listing is available at: www.cambridge.org/EPOR

For EU product safety concerns, contact us at Calle de José Abascal, 56–1°,
28003 Madrid, Spain or eugpsr@cambridge.org.

www.ingramcontent.com/pod-product-compliance
Lightning Source LLC
LaVergne TN
LVHW020350260326
834688LV00045B/1642